Crown

of

Glory

Receiving the Lord's Blessings by Becoming an Overcomer

by Leslie Johnson

You are an Overcomer!. God Bless!. Leslie

1

Crown of Glory

All Scripture quotations are taken from the
Authorized King James Version of the Bible

Printed in the United States of America

Cover photo furnished by
PRIVILEGE ORFEVRERIE
10 Rue Demarquay 75010
Paris, France

ISBN #1-58538-017-2

Leslie Johnson
Spirit of Prophecy Church
P. O. Box 750234
Topeka, KS 66675

e-mail at lesliej@cjnetworks.com
Phone: 785-266-1112

2

Forward

This is a great privilege to be able to write the forward to this work having been part of the prophetic presbytery that was ministering to Leslie Johnson when this book "birthed." Truly we were in a heavenly atmosphere surrounded by angels and the weight of God's glory was upon us as we began to prophesy. As Leslie will expound through her excellent style of writing, suddenly I saw a crown appear over her head and the Lord said, "This is a crown of Glory and Honor."

I've looked back to that event numerous times pondering what the Lord meant by "a crown of Glory and Honor." Several times I have ministered side by side with Leslie and Stan Johnson, and know their love for the Lord. I've seen their faith in action, I know the fruit of the Spirit that has been imparted and now reflects through the lives of three of their four children I have met but... "What was this crown over Leslie all about?"

As you will learn through this book, a crown is symbolic of authority. I believe that Leslie has received authority to release an anointing of righteousness that will prepare the Body of Christ to receive God's glory. As the glory is restored, so will honor be restored, and the Church will arise.

As you read this book, you will laugh, you will cry, you will wonder, you will repent, you will yell, "Thank you Jesus!" Leslie's prophetic anointing will cut to your heart, and then her practical wisdom will restore your hope as your faith grows and you see yourself as an "overcomer."

This is an important book for anyone who wants to please the Lord in this end-time hour. The words will challenge you and "wash" you as you respond to the spirit of righteousness. I pray the Lord gives you "ears to hear" and enlarges your heart to walk in His blessings as you seek to please Him in every area of life.

Patrick Sparrow
Capstone Ministries International

Dedication

I would like to thank you, Stan Johnson, my wonderful husband, for being the spiritual leader you are in our home. You truly portray what the true minister of the home is all about. You have encouraged me. You have given me opportunities to learn, grow in the Lord, and to speak to many people. Without your persistence and trust in me, I would never have been able to accomplish the things in life that have been handed to me. You have been like the cheerleader on the sides, getting me pepped up and ready to rumble! You are a man of your word, a teacher, an encourager, and provider of many opportunities. You are a man who promotes others in the Kingdom of God. May the Lord richly bless you for not only helping me and giving me opportunities, but all the hundreds of others you have helped train and equip for Endtime ministries. I consider it an awesome blessing, honor and privilege to be your wife and the one who gets to sleep with you each night.

Thank you Stan; I love you!
^more

Leslie Johnson

Contents

The Crowning Moment

Imagine, walking along a winding road,
When you see a kingdom made of **Gold**.
Do you choose to go in?

On with your journey you continue to toil,
As you search for that **Anointing Oil**.
Do you quench your spirit?

The next horizon tells a sweet story,
Of our Savior who came from **Glory**.
Do you watch the Son?

Around the way you feel forlorn,
You find the rose with many **Thorns**.
Do you stop and smell?

Love for the Lord a bird is voicing,
You can sense his level of **Rejoicing**.
Do you join in the song?

You see His cross of unselfishness,
You suddenly feel His **Righteousness**.
Do you go on your way?

You reach the end and remember the strife,
You look back and think of your whole **Life**.
Do you have regrets?

You can choose to pass these crowns on by,
Or you can raise them to our Lord on **High**.
The choice is yours.

samantha wilson

Chapter 1

A Visitation from the Throne Room of God

Revelation 3:21 ___To him that overcometh will I grant___ ___to sit with me in my throne, even as I also overcame,___ ___and am set down with my Father in his throne.___

It was an evening full of praise and worship, and the Spirit of the Lord was so very strong and powerful. Three prophets of God were in the room and began to speak the Word of the Lord and prophesy to my husband, Stan. Soon I found myself being brought to the front to be prophesied to as well. When the prophets finished speaking to my husband, one of them began to speak the following Word from the Lord to me:

> "The Lord says, 'Daughter, I am undergirding you
> with strength. You know some things. God has told you

7

some deep things. You are taking on a new identity in Me,' says the Lord. 'You are different than what you used to be. In the next few years, you are going to become more different. You are really going to step into your own ministry for the Kingdom. Still together with your husband, but you are really going to take your own in your own ministry.' God has got a place of power and a place of the Word, and 'I am going to adorn you with My Word and with My power,' says God. 'With the Word of the Lord, it is going to flow out through your mouth, and it is going to be gracious unto them that hear it. It is going to bring health, life, and healing to those who hear it. There are several more books you are going to be writing. You will sit down sometimes, and it is just going to flow. It will not be a hard thing; it is not going to be a difficult thing; it is just going to flow. You are going to be a tremendous blessing to the women everywhere I send you. I want you to be thinking about women's meetings, some women's conferences, and women's seminars. Plan a time that you can get them together. A time that you can refresh my daughters. A time you can impart in them hope and life.'

"The Lord says, 'You have seen some women who have despair and no hope. It is in your heart to be able to lift them up and revive them. I am going to give you the wherewithal to be able to do it. There will be times you gather women together, and it will be like a women's conference. There will be a gift that you will give the women, a meaningful gift that you will be able to give to absolutely every single person that attends. You will be a blessing to those who attend.' 'But,' the Lord says, 'You are taking on My identity more and more and more and your identity is in Me,' says the Lord."

At this point, I was having a difficult time standing because of the anointing of the Lord. Another prophet began to prophesy to me. I

8

remember hearing one word, and that word was "crown".

> The prophet of God said, "I just saw a crown, a crown
> to be put upon you. The Lord says, 'Daughter, I crown you
> with glory and honor. I am releasing more of My power and
> more of My anointing on you.'"

When I heard the word "*crown*", I was slain in the spirit because of the anointing of God. This may not make sense to some. That is okay. When you have experienced the anointing of the Lord, His presence surrounding you, you also will have a difficult time standing up! This is not an area we want to disagree upon, I am just telling you what happened to me. I pray the Lord's anointing will be present in all who read this book. I want you to experience what I have with the Lord.

I remember during this time of "floor ministry" being at such peace with God. During this time of being ministered to by the Lord, I also remember asking Him a lot of questions. The Lord responded by saying, "sh, sh, be quiet my darling." At that moment, I felt a lot of things begin to happen. All of a sudden, there was like an electrical surge shooting through my body. I also had the sensation of a small breeze blowing over me. There was no way I could even attempt to get up. I felt like I was glued to one spot on the floor.

> With such peacefulness, the Lord said, "I have two
> more books for you to write." At that moment, I saw two
> covers. The first one was a big, red ruby. It was pure, transpar-
> ent, and beautiful. He said, "I want you to write about being
> 'More Than A Ruby.' This book will be directed specifically to
> 'My beautiful daughters.'" The second image the Lord showed
> me was the most beautiful crown you could imagine. A golden
> crown I could not even begin to describe. This crown was
> more beautiful than could possibly be depicted on the cover
> of this book. The jewels were of different colors, and the gold

9

was so brilliant in its luster. The Lord said, "Write the book and title it *'Crown of Glory.'*" He further said, "I want My children to be overcomers."

Many who witnessed this event in my life declared that I was on the floor, slain in the Spirit, under the anointing of the Lord, for over an hour. The prophets said that they saw a beautiful crown from heaven come down and the Lord placing it upon my head. That is when the Spirit of the Living Lord anointed me. The next day, these three prophets of God all felt impressed to anoint me with oil and impart the prophetic anointing to me and ordain me as a prophetess. I have not been the same since. When someone anoints you, it is like receiving a white belt; but when they ordain you, it is like receiving a black belt in Karate.

After this experience, I began to ask the Lord, "What do you mean crown of glory and honor?" I had a lot of thoughts running through my mind, so I first began to meditate about crowns. A crown, according to *Webster's Dictionary*, is "a garland or wreath worn on the head as a sign of honor and victory." If a crown is placed on someone's head, it is a reward or honor given for the position or title of a champion. A crown often has gold and jewels and is worn as an emblem of sovereignty. A crown can also mean the summit or highest point, as of a mountain. Another meaning of crown is that it is also the lowest point of an anchor, between the arms. To be crowned is to have a position of the highest rank. By receiving this position, a person would be considered enormously successful. Also, when a crown is placed on someone's head, it is in effect putting the finishing touch on them denoting their position or royalty.

The crown is also described as a form of protection. An analogy to this would involve the importance of tooth enamel. The enamel's function is to protect and cover the tooth. Enamel also keeps the tooth from decaying. If you go to a dentist to receive a crown on the tooth, the crown is there for protection and to guard against sensitivity to heat and cold. Just the thought of not having that protection on my teeth sends a cold chill down my spine. In a similar vein, I cannot imagine how people make it without the Lord. We need to realize just how much He does protect us. If we get into self-pity and self-destruction, we lose sight of what really matters. Ask the Lord to bring to your remembrance a time that He recently protected you. You may be surprised how constant that protection really is!

Since a crown also represents the highest point of a mountain, receiving a crown from the Lord would represent the highest point one can reach in the Lord's Kingdom. With our next definition, when we are at our lowest point, the Lord, of course, is our anchor. On an anchor, the portion between the two arms is the heaviest one. An anchor of a ship holds the ship in place, even when there are waves moving it back and forth. This is what Jesus does for us: He holds us up and also holds us in place so we do not stumble, fall, or move. When the waves keep rolling in, threatening to drown us during the rough times in our lives, our Anchor (Jesus) keeps us from floating and drifting far away. He is the one who keeps us secure.

The Bible says in Ephesians, Chapter Four; that when Jesus ascended up on high, He led captivity captive and gave gifts to all men. In other words, He stopped the captive from being taken into captivity. Also, He that descended is the same One who ascended up above the heavens that He would fulfill all things. The Lord's children should always be growing in the awareness of the glory of Christ. This is not just head knowledge; it is about experiencing the fullness of Christ. From the mountaintop to the lowest part of the earth, Jesus has the ultimate crowns to bestow on us. When we receive them, they will take a hold, be secure, and not able to be displaced by man.

Hebrews 6:18-20 *That by two immutable things, in which it was impossible for God to lie, we might have a strong consolation, who have fled for refuge to lay hold upon the hope set before us: Which hope we have as an anchor of the soul, both sure and stedfast, and which entereth into that within the veil; Whither*

11

the forerunner is for us entered, even Jesus, made an high priest for ever after the order of Melchisedec.

Glory of the Lord

The word *"glory"* means great honor and admiration obtained by someone doing something important or valuable. It is anything that brings the Lord worshipful adoration or praise. Glory also denotes the highest achievement, splendor, and prosperity. It is a symbol of radiant beauty, splendor, and magnificence. Glory is synonymous with heaven or the bliss of heaven. Biblical scholars and the Word of God tells us that when the glory of the Lord appeared, it was like a cloud. Also, according to another description of glory, it is a circle of light. If someone is filled with glory it means they are being very proud, filled with rejoicing and exultation, and feeling their best, and happiest.

I recently conducted a women's conference called *"The Perfect Touch."* During the morning praise and worship session, there were ladies dancing and singing praises to our King. The women at this conference were all in such unity and exuded tremendous love for the Lord. That evening, one of the ladies attending the conference told me, "One of the employees of the hotel stopped me and began to ask questions about the conference." She was full of excitement and questions. The hotel employee asked one of the women in attendance, "Were you one of the dancers in the back of the room?" My friend Myra replied, "Yes, I was dancing in the back, why?" She said, "I heard the music and all the singing and I was curious, so I peeked in the window of the conference room door. I saw a strange thing, though. I saw what looked like a bright light surrounding all the dancers, and it was covering everyone all the way to the front of the room. It was like this cloud was in the room."

Over the next several hours, two more employees mentioned that they had seen the same thing at different times. When the glory of the Lord enters a room, it is like a cloud or a bright light. When we praise Him with our whole being and desire His presence, isn't it awesome what the Lord will do? These three employees of the hotel were not saved. They were unbelievers coming to look in the conference room because they were curious. The Lord opened their eyes to see His glory!

1 Kings 8:11 *So that the priests could not stand to minister because of the cloud: for the glory of the LORD had filled the house of the LORD.*

Honor, connotes being worthy of esteem. High regard or great respect is given, received, or enjoyed when honor is bestowed upon someone. To be honored, one must have a good reputation. A person with honor will have a keen sense of what is right and wrong and possess integrity. To have honor, there needs to be chastity or purity in the person's life. A man of honor will receive a high-ranking position, distinction, and recognition. Honor is a title of respect when given to a person as in judges having the title "Your Honor". When someone has honor, a badge, token, or an act of respect may be given to that person.

When you think of someone who is honored, you think that person or action has brought great respect and fame to a school, country, church, or kingdom. When someone with honor enters a room, people will automatically show great respect, high regard for them, and will treat them with deference. Have you ever been around someone who carries this kind of authority? My dad was a man whom people really respected and honored. He would just walk in a room and people would automatically begin to serve him out of a deep sense of respect. There was just something about him that demanded respect. He did not demand respect...it just happened.

To honor can also mean to worship. Someone who has great honor will be faithful to carry out the terms of an assignment. If we were found to be honorable, we would be accepted as valid and good. If honor is a goal, then what is at stake is one's good name, truthfulness, trustworthiness, or reliability. Deference suggests a display of courteous regard for a

13

superior or for one to whom respect is due, by yielding to the person's status, claims, or wishes. Deference is given to one who is honored.

When a crown of glory and honor is given to us, the children of the living God, this means we would receive the reward of a high position in the Kingdom of God. In order to receive this crown, we must fulfill our obligations and be reliable. We also would have to possess a keen sense of what is good and right. Therefore, I believe it is beneficial for each one of us to strive for that honor. If we desire to be crowned with His glory and honor, then ultimately we must desire true holiness and righteousness. This involves a day-to-day walk and communication with the Lord. When the Lord finds us worthy of receiving His crowns, a protection inevitably accompanies it.

In the Word of God, there are many verses about crowns. Crowns are given to us when we receive Jesus as Lord and Savior; thus, we receive them when we have eternal life. However, there are spiritual crowns we can desire and strive to receive while we are here on earth, not just once we enter heaven. As I was researching crowns for this book, I desired to know which ones the Lord would give His children, and how we achieve them.

The Different Crowns the Word of God Lists

The following list of crowns are delineated in the Word:

1   **The Crown of Gold. Will Receive at His appearing.**

2   **The Crown of Anointing Oil. Spiritual crown to be received now.**

3   **The Crown of Glory. (Sometimes called Crown of Glory and Honor). Represents gaining wisdom. We can re-**

ceive the spiritual crown of glory now, but if not, we will definitely receive this crown at His appearing.

4   The Crown of Thorns. The crown Jesus wore.

5   The Crown of Rejoicing. Will receive at His appearing, but we may also receive this crown when someone is saved.

6   The Crown of Righteousness. Will receive at His appearing.

7   The Crown of Life. Will receive at His appearing.

Remember, when Jesus Christ reappears, we His followers, His children, His Bride will receive a crown of glory that will never be removed. Hallelujah!

1 Peter 5:4 *And when the chief Shepherd shall appear, ye shall receive a crown of glory that fadeth not away.*

15

Crown of Glory

Chapter 2

Take Home the Gold

Psalms 21:1-3 *The king shall joy in thy strength, O LORD; and in thy salvation how greatly shall he rejoice! <u>Thou hast given him his heart's desire</u>, and hast not withholden the request of his lips. Selah. For thou preventest him with the blessings of goodness: <u>thou settest a crown of pure gold on his head</u>.*

Over the years, I have had the opportunity, as well as the pleasure, of seeing our daughter, Leslie Ann, receive many crowns. At last count, she has won over 65 crowns and many more trophies. She won these awards in a period of about three years. Some of the crowns and tiaras she managed to win were very large, and others were small. Some of the crowns have different colored jewels, and some are simply decorated with either gold or

17

silver with Austrian crystals (which look like diamonds).

As I began to write this book, I reflected about how Leslie Ann won these crowns. One reason I know she received so many awards is because she is an extremely talented young woman. More importantly it was the result of her working very diligently and being very dedicated. Even though she was quite young at the time, Leslie Ann kept her focus and determination. I also recognized that at a very early age our daughter demonstrated that she was very goal oriented. I remember when she was only two years old, she saw modeling shows and she exclaimed, "Mommy, I want to do that! I want to be on stage." Immediately I thought, "No way! We are a Christian family and you will do no such thing." She would also say, "Mommy, I want to be a movie star." I was about to discover that when the Lord gives the desire to someone, no matter what their age, there is no way of changing the plans God has established for their life.

Stan and I went to a Full Gospel Business Men's meeting one evening. We had our two youngest children there with us. Leslie Ann was only two years old and had fallen asleep during the meeting. At the end of the service the gentleman speaking called Stan and I up to the front. He began to prophesy to us, when all of a sudden he went in a completely different direction and began to prophesy over Leslie Ann.

He said, "I have anointed her with the ashes of beauty. She will be used for My glory. I will cause many to be drawn to her. I will make her known all over the world. She has been called to praise me in song."

At that moment I really had no concept what the Lord was actually saying.

Isaiah 61:3 *To <u>appoint</u> unto them that mourn in Zion, to give unto them beauty for ashes, the oil of joy for mourning, the garment of praise for the spirit of heaviness; that they might be called trees of righteousness, the*

planting of the LORD, that he might be glorified.

In addition, we were visiting a church for the second time when Leslie Ann was four years old and a woman approached me at the end of the service. She remarked, "You have a very beautiful daughter. Have you ever thought about getting her into modeling or pageants?" I was shocked. I had already been trying to avoid this avenue for the last two years. I thought, "How can I get out of this conversation?" I replied, "I have thought about it, but I have no way of knowing how to get information about pageants or modeling." I thought to myself. *"Whew, that was close."* To my dismay, this woman responded, "I have information about a pageant coming to town, and I am a modeling coach. I would like Leslie Ann in my class." She gave me the details about the pageant I could enter Leslie Ann in; so I gave in. My daughter came alive on stage! I could not believe that was my child. She took home the gold, and I even knew then that she was meant to be on stage.

A couple of weeks later, a woman approached us in the grocery store where we were shopping. She began, "I know you do not know me, but I was a judge at the pageant your daughter was in a couple of weeks ago. I would like to tell you something your daughter said to me." My immediate thought was, *"Oh no, what embarrassing thing did Leslie Ann say?"* She continued, "I asked Leslie Ann what she wanted to be when she grew up. She answered, 'I want to be a movie star, but with a pretty heart, because I have Jesus in my heart. DO YOU?'" The woman concluded, "She had my total vote from that moment on. I am a Christian, and I was so taken by her boldness, especially in a four year old." You see, I needed to hear those words. At that moment I realized, God's children need to be on television shows, the radio, and become the well-known movie stars and singers. What a wonderful way to get the world to listen to the gospel! Unfortunately, as in so many other areas, we have let down our guard and allowed the evil of the world to rise up and take over, because we are "too spiritual" to do such things.

There were times when Leslie Ann would compete and not come

home with a crown. Once in awhile I noted her disappointment, but the majority of the time she would come home from the competition as if she were the winner. As I wondered how such a young woman could have such a good attitude, I realized that whether she won that crown or not, if she felt like she did a good job and did her best, she was perfectly content not receiving a crown. However, if she felt like she did not do her best, then she would become disappointed and upset with herself. Not once did I see her jealous of another contestant, she was always happy for the winner. Even being upset with herself was short-lived and she became more determined than ever to win the crown the next time around. Leslie Ann would conclude that she needed to become even more focused and determined for the next competition. I would find her practicing hours on end to make sure she hit every note of her song and every dance move was just perfect. Not only did she work very hard on her own, but also she sought out help from those who were the "best." She then practiced continuously so that every movement she made was like the "best". Sometimes I found that she had practiced so diligently that she would perform the best contestant whole modeling routine exactly as they would, down to the minute details.

Are you beginning to see the pattern for what the Lord wants from us in His kingdom? He wants us to be focused, determined, work hard and never give up. The Lord doesn't want us to get upset if we mess up, He just wants us to try again. As children of the Most High God, we are to have high morals and integrity. We are to watch our mouths and attitudes. We are to continue to strive to be like the "best." Think of someone you know whom you respect and honor. You also recognize that they desire God's perfect will more than you do. Watch how they act, what they do and what words come out of their mouth. Work toward being like them in the areas you're weak. The only perfect One was Jesus, and it must be our highest goal to be like Him.

With being involved in the "pageant" programs with our daughter and other endeavors of my own, I've found that most of the time when the judging is fair, the best contestant wins. Also, I have noticed that the audience does not necessarily always agree with the judge's choice. Likewise, we won't always be popular with the world, but our righteous judge will select His chosen ones. This is the way our crowns are laid up for us in the kingdom of heaven. Our Lord Jesus is a righteous judge, and His ways are fair and just. We do not always understand His ways or timing. One thing we can count on is that He will guide us to the next level, whether we want to go there or not.

When someone wears a crown, whether it is awarded or because they come from a royal lineage, their integrity is of the utmost importance. Whoever wins the Miss America title, for example, will travel across America promoting her platform as well as many of the organization's positions. She must hold to a high moral standard or she will be asked to relinquish her crown. We have already seen this occur during the history of the Miss America program. To keep the crown, there are rules to follow, contracts to be signed, regulations, long hours, dedication, and high standards that are required of the winner and must be maintained.

Parents, we are responsible to raise our children in the nurture and admonition of the Lord. We can experience no greater joy than when our children grow up to serve Jesus. Everyone with children feel that their child is the most beautiful, the most precious of all. It doesn't matter whether it is a boy or a girl. During the pageants, it would be such a conflict when I would see a beautiful child all clean, hair in place, wearing stunning clothing and being friendly. Then I would see the parent looking completely different. He or she would be filthy, their clothes didn't even match, their hair was a mess and they were being rude to the other parents and children. It didn't make sense to me.

The Lord showed me that many of us are like these parents who are consumed by the fear that their child would not look his/her best. Many of us are so busy looking at what is right or wrong with everyone else; that we fail to take a look at our own behavior and attitude. Instead of being so preoccupied with others, if we examined ourselves then maybe we would be better witnesses for Christ. Too many times we look and point the finger at someone else instead of checking out our own robes of

21

righteousness to assure that they are clean.

The press all over the world scrutinizes royalty. For example, in England they are watched and covered in the newscasts concerning everything that they do. If they make a mistake or sin, the whole world will be notified of the situation and they are judged. Every newspaper, tabloid, and magazine details the horrible scandals. Whether Royalty, Miss America, or Miss USA, they all must watch what they eat, how they dress, and how they interact and speak with people. They must have manners, integrity, and high morals. Once they receive the prized crown, they are known for that position and title the rest of their lives. Even when the title is taken away by the authorities, as in the case of Princess Diana, she was and always will be considered a favorite beautiful Princess among many. The hierarchy might have physically removed her crown and title; however, because of her influence and work, the world will always know her as the beautiful "Princess Diana."

Remember; once you receive your crown / crowns, no one can ever take them away from you. You have received a crown from the Most High God.

Revelation 3:11 *Behold, I come quickly: hold that fast which thou hast, that <u>no man take thy crown.</u>*

Chapter 3

Will You Receive a Crown?

1 Peter 5:4 *And when the chief Shepherd shall appear, ye shall receive a crown of glory that fadeth not away.*

We must be mindful that there needs to be a realization from us that there are certain requirements in order for us to receive a crown. Integrity and honor are of the utmost importance. The Lord requires that we not defile others or ourselves. We are to stay pure and not use our own bodies in any way that would be displeasing to our Lord. In today's society, it is very common to see young people, as well as we who are older and supposedly more mature, living in sin. We do not think anything about living together before marriage, having sex outside of marriage,

23

cursing one another, engaging in the use of pornography, masturbating, divorcing, having abortions, gambling, etc. We think piercing our bodies wherever we desire is perfectly permissible. We think tattooing our body all over is fine, never bothering to ask the Lord what He thinks about it.

It used to be frowned upon if a man and woman were living together. Now if two women or two men are roommates, then rumors fly that they must be homosexuals. Our society looks with greater favor on sexual sin then abstinence. Our young people in society today are confused. They don't want to be looked upon as if something is wrong with them, when they have pure motives and are trying to do what is right. If they are young Christians and have roommates of the same sex, they find themselves appearing to others as if they are doing something evil and sinful, even if they are not.

If we desire to be priests unto our King, then we need to keep ourselves from defiling our bodies, as well as those of others. The word defile means to make unclean or impure. It also means to corrupt the purity or perfection of someone or something. Sexual perversion is rampant in our world. Unfortunately, we see this even in our Christian churches. There are divorces, sodomy, fornication, and all kinds of evil practices evident even in Christian families. There are not only actual acts of homosexuality and lesbianism, but sexual fantasies of this nature are entertained by Christian's minds. People think that they are hiding their secret sins, but in reality they are not hidden at all.

Feminism has perverted what womanhood is all about. A perverse spirit has entered this nation and we have even allowed a spirit of Jezebel to rise up. Who was Jezebel? Jezebel was a worshiper of Baal. She was a wicked woman who usurped the rule of Israel for about thirty years. Ahab, her husband, was a wimp and had no backbone to stand up to his wife. As a matter of fact, he **liked** her ability to manipulate her subjects. This was a way for him to get what he wanted as well. Jezzie was full of sexual immorality and not only allowed this type of perversion, but also encouraged such practices in her kingdom. Someone with a Jezebel spirit, whether male or female, will have impure motives and seek out others to follow them. Someone with this spirit will be eager to gain control and desire to "teach" others. Once they begin to deceive their followers, they desire to gain credibility, and thus appear to many to be the most spiritual person in the church. A person with a Jezebel spirit is not always easily recognized. Many times this person will conjure up dreams, visions, prophetic words and insight in order to be recognized. Once they are recognized and someone discerns the presence of this spirit, the person will become very agitated and deny any wrongdoing. Once asked to leave, they will take many with them, for they desire to divide in order to conquer. The sooner this sinful, controlling person is revealed, the fewer people will be affected.

I believe we had a Jezebel in the White House not long ago. She desired to take control and manipulate many others to get her way. We now see this same woman as Senator of a state. After leaving the White House, she was going to make sure she still had some control. This woman has a strong feminist viewpoint and believes that feminism was the philosophy American women should embrace. Nowadays, we ladies don't even know what it means to be feminine. Because of the tremendous upsurge of feminism, we see that men do not know how to be a gentleman either. The way I see it, feminism is actually the way the lesbians have gained power. Think about it. They originated Planned Parenthood. The lesbians and those practicing feminism are actually the women who probably don't want children in the first place, so that is why they fight for abortion rights. We have become so "rights"- oriented in this country that we do not even know what is right or wrong anymore.

Someone busy fighting for their "rights" often appear to think others do not have the right to voice their opinion. I remember once in Toronto, Canada, we were sitting at an outside cafe. There were some pretty weird people walking up and down this street. It was certainly entertaining. A young man and woman came near where we were sitting, and they looked absolutely disgusting. Their hair was spiked straight up and multicolored. They were both wearing a lot of makeup and all black clothes. I got my camera and took a picture of them, and at this

25

they went berserk. I thought they were going to hit me! A friend of ours got in between them and me and stopped them from attacking me. I said to them, "Well, obviously you want to draw attention to yourself or you would not dress that way." They were of the opinion that how they dressed and acted was fine, but I wasn't allowed to have an opinion.

Homosexuals hold the opinion that what they are doing is perfectly all right. But, if we give voice to the opposite opinion then we are wrong. It's the same way with those who want an abortion. They feel that what they do is their business, and no one should voice their disapproval. I beg to differ. If someone is allowing my country to shed innocent blood resulting in judgment coming on our land because of their sin, you can bet that I will state my objection!

A Jezebel has many evil spirits controlling them to make sure their plans are fulfilled. We saw a controlling spirit, seducing spirit, anti-Christ spirit, lying spirit, spirit of error, perverse spirit, and spirit of deception all rise to power in the White House. The Jezebel spirit will give legal rights to homosexuals and feminist, and will utilize divination and manipulation to accomplish these objectives. All these manifestations of evil that arrive are doors opened in the spiritual realm. Because that door was opened to this perverted spirit in the White House, it is still in control of the White House now. A Jezebel spirit will not only avoid righteousness, but will deny it.

There is probably a little bit of a Jezebel spirit in all of us, if we honestly look at our lives in terms of our actions, attitudes and personality. We need to be on our faces daily praying for this wonderful nation the Lord has allows us to live in. It is just as important to be praying daily to see if there are any manifestations of a Jezebel spirit in our own lives. If there are, we must earnestly ask the Lord to remove and cast out that manifestation. Some manifestations of a Jezebel spirit are listed below.

One who has a Jezebel spirit will:

Betray, bribe, deceive, act as a decoy, entice, entrap, hook, lead astray, lead on, lure mislead, persuade, rope in, captivate, charm, come on to, tempt, and or be flirtatious and distracting.

1 Timothy 4:1 *Now the Spirit speaketh expressly, that in the latter times some shall depart from the faith, giving heed to seducing spirits, and doctrines of devils;*

Sexual Perversion

I asked to borrow a dictionary from my friend to look up the definition of feminism, but I couldn't find the word. I examined the first page and saw that the dictionary was published in 1961. Obviously, feminism was unknown at the time of that printing. We Christians have allowed so many tragic things to happen in our society. If Christian women had stood up and protested as this movement started up, maybe the world would still believe that being **feminine is okay.** I love being a woman and being feminine. I enjoy being the "weaker" vessel. It is a safe place, not a place of disrespect.

A friend of mine told me recently that she has noticed in the high school where she teaches that more and more young girls are not feminine anymore. As a matter of fact, they do not want anything to do with being "ladylike". She asked me, "What is happening to the women in our country? We are not ladies, and we certainly are not feminine." She continued, "I have one particular young woman in my class who rebels even against the word feminine. When she comes into class, she props her feet up on her desk, slouches down in the chair, and smacks her gum." I tell her every day, "Jenny, please take your feet off the desk! The way you are sitting isn't very ladylike. Jenny's response day after day is, "I'm not a lady, and I don't want to be!" We must get back to the Word of God and recognize our place. The Scriptures tell us that the more seasoned women of God are to teach the younger ones. It has to start somewhere, it might as well begin with you!

Not long ago, I was teaching on the subject of how and why a man needs to keep his future wife pure. A man is not to commit fornication

27

with a woman. A man of God should respect a woman enough to keep her pure before marriage. The Lord has made man head over the woman, so it is the man's responsibility to keep the woman pure. God will hold him responsible, because he is the one who is supposedly the "stronger" vessel. The man is the one who God put in charge over the woman.

1 Corinthians 11:3 *But I would have you know, that the head of every man is Christ; and the <u>head of the woman is the man;</u> and the head of Christ is God.*

Are You Sexually Pure?

Once at a meeting I was teaching about sexual purity between men and women. An older gentleman, perhaps around 70 years old, came up and informed me that once you have sex with a woman, then you marry her in the eyes of God and that getting a marriage license was illegal. He continued, "Therefore, it is not fornication that people commit, but it is legal in God's eyes." To say the least, I was appalled. If you know me you know I had a reaction to this man and to post the following question. I asked, "Then why does God put so much emphasis on fleeing from fornication and adultery? Also, why is marriage so important to God?" As the Bride of Christ our relationship with Jesus is likened to marriage. I was shocked that first of all, a man of his age would actually think this was the correct way of thinking, and second in that to him, living together was okay! I looked over at this man's wife and saw such hurt and bitterness inside her. She had a huge frown upon her face and looked so hard and uncaring. I could tell that she was a very miserable woman.

The "prophetess" in me came to the forefront. I told him, "You need to repent and ask forgiveness, not only of the Lord, but of your wife also. I do <u>not</u> mean to wait and speak to her tomorrow, you better do it now!" Women, whether we realize it or not, we hold anger in our heart against a man who has defiled us. This man was trying to justify his actions and sin rather than admit his guilt and ask forgiveness. Isn't this what we as Christians often do? When we have done something wrong, committed some kind of sin against our Lord, we try to justify our actions, rather than take responsibility for them and repent.

I confess that my husband and I had sex before we were married. We not only hurt our Lord through this sin, but hurt each other. I had given in to the temptation and the lust of my flesh, just like my husband. Unfortunately, most marriages are really the result of the lust and don't originate in the heavenly throne room of God. It usually takes years of growing and maturing in the Word together to definitely say that the Lord is the center of our marriage. If we continue to live a married life only in the flesh, difficulties will arise. I truly felt as though I had agreed to this temptation and tried to rationalize out our actions. It became clear early in our marriage that we loved each other, but did we marry because of lust? Those questions would enter my mind, and I had to cast them out. I really loved this man and desired to spend eternity with him, but there was something hurting inside of me.

After several years of marriage, Stan and I went to a marriage seminar. On the second day of the conference the program director said, "Today we are going to talk about submission." My thought was "Oh, great! Just what I want to hear." In those days I truly hated that word! Early on in our marriage, Stan would use the "S" word against me to get whatever he wanted done. In his eyes, I was not a "good" wife, a "submitted" wife if I didn't do everything he wanted. Obviously, my concepts that I was this precious princess of his and I should have whatever I wanted were completely wrong. He was supposed to be this prince who came riding in on his white horse and worshipped the ground I walked on. However, I was so stubborn, strong willed that if he told me to jump, I would put my hands on my hips and say, "You jump and I will tell YOU how high!" I did not like being ordered around, and I sure didn't want to sit there and hear about the "submission" word from another man. Yuk!

I was squirming in my seat ready to make an exit. Fortunately I began to listen to what the man had to say, "Men, if you want submission from your wife, then first many of you need to ask forgiveness for defiling her body before marriage. She holds a grudge in her heart against you, whether you realize it or not. If you had sex with her before you took her hand in marriage, then there is anger bubbling over in her heart against you." At that moment, I searched my heart and decided that yes, I had some bitterness and anger against my husband, but it couldn't be because of that! I mean... I was in on this sinful act too. I remember making a conscious decision at the time we committed fornication that it was okay with me. At least I think I did. All these thoughts were racing through my mind. I mean, I seduced him as much. The justifications and rationalizations went around and around in my head. We sat there and listened to this man speak about how it was the man's responsibility to keep the woman pure. *(Now ladies, I am not giving you an excuse for a way out of taking responsibility for the sin you committed).*

As we continued to listen to the speaker, I couldn't wait for the break so I could get away and really check my heart. Finally, the moment came when he said, "We will take a ten-minute break." As soon as he said this, Stan took my hand and wouldn't let me up. I turned to him and was about to ask him, "What are you doing?" My wonderful husband had me look directly into his eyes. He got down on one knee, took my other hand in his, and with tears rolling down his cheeks, he said, "Leslie, please forgive me. I have done you wrong, and I took advantage of you. You are so special and precious to me, yet I committed a terrible sin against you, and I want you to forgive me. Will you forgive me?" My response, at least what I thought was about to come out of my mouth was, "Oh, its okay, I wanted to do that also." Instead, all I got out of my mouth was, "Oh, its...." before I burst into tears and cried in my husband's arms to what seemed like a very long time. You see, I <u>had</u> held bitterness and anger in my heart against Stan and I didn't even know it. As a matter of fact, I would be absolutely furious with him and not know why.

The reason we need to get clean regarding this sexual sin issue is that before a man can love his wife as Christ loves the church, and before the woman can reverence her husband, issues like this need to be resolved. You see submission is easy when both the husband and the wife are clean and treating each other in a biblical manner. When a man is servant to his wife and treats her like a queen, then the woman automatically responds and submits. When she feels secure and loved then there is no need to rebel and isolate herself.

There are 40 Scriptures in the Bible on the issue of fornication alone. We, the church have done great injustice in the area of marriage. Whether or not you want to get a license from the state or not is your business; however, the church is to recognize the marriage between two people. Are they both saved? Are they walking the walk and talking the talk of the Bible? Are they pure and holy? It is the church's responsibility to continue encouraging and expecting our engaged couples to stay pure and innocent. Too many times sin is overlooked in the church. We are afraid of "offending" someone. Most of the time the leaders of a church body would rather have someone in their midst continue in their sinful state than to confront or embarrass them. Is this the right attitude?

Several times before couples have gotten married in our church, the Lord has revealed their sexual sin to me. I go directly to them and tell them, "This is what the Lord says you are doing. You are committing sin and you need to stop, repent, ask forgiveness, and not commit fornication again." I think too many times our preachers are too shy, or perhaps too wimpy, to speak openly and sincerely with couples and let them know of this sin's consequences. Probably one reason they don't do this is because they fornicated before they were married, and don't want to deal with the "problem", (really sin issue) themselves. If we are to receive a crown of righteousness from our Lord, <u>then</u> we need to stop sinning and turn to the Lord with our "whole" heart, body, soul and spirit. We need to determine in our minds and hearts that righteousness and holiness are what we want.

I had a young man in our church say to me, "Did you know that 90 percent or more of couples even in the church commit fornication?"

31

This is not a very comforting thought but probably an accurate statement. The problem is that the Church has begun to justify this act of sin instead of confront the issue. Many believers in Jesus Christ justify their actions, since they believe so many other Christians are doing the same things.

A young man recently wanted to speak to me; he was in love with a young woman attending our youth group. The young woman had a child out of wedlock with another man, but he loved her and her child. I will call this young man David. David originally came to speak to me about all kinds of problems in his life; from finances, to a place to live, to getting a car, to health, and so forth. As he began to unload all of his problems, I asked him, "Are you and (I'll call her Sabrina) living together?" They were. I asked David, "If you love her and the baby so much, then why won't you marry her?" David replied, "I want to. We are planning on getting married in about a year." I said, "Why are you waiting? Let us marry you and Sabrina; let's get the sin out of your lives and see things turn around for you both." His response was, "I'm ready now. I want to marry Sabrina. I want to do things right, but she wants to have a big wedding. So we need to plan and save our money." My response was not a popular one. "She already has a child out of wedlock, you and she are living together in sin, and you need to make things right with God. Righteousness and holiness are more important than a big wedding. She had her opportunity to make things right months ago, but she messed up... we all do in some area or another. Right now, let's make your life right with the Lord. Tell her we will help her with the wedding plans and if you two are to marry, then we can put this together quickly." I also told him, "In the meantime, between now and the day of your marriage, you need to move out of the house and prepare a place for her. Desire to keep her pure. Repent now, and we will help."

As David left, he wanted to become clean once again. He longed to marry this young, beautiful woman. He was going to tell her that evening the plans he had. I heard through another young couple at our church that Sabrina became very upset with him for ruining her fantasy. Her plan was to live together for the next year, save their money for a big wedding, which would include her wearing a white wedding gown, him wearing a tuxedo, and all the rest of the things that go along with a dream wedding. She was angry that someone from the church would even mention forgetting the big, formal wedding. David succumbed to the grip of the devil once again. This young woman began playing on David's emotion and manipulating to get her way. David did not want to rock the boat; he was caught up in the pleasure of having sex and playing house. Instead of being a righteous man and moving out, he decided to stay where he was comfortable. That was sad.

This is where the Church is today. We would rather stay in our filthy rags because we are comfortable, than to put on clean, freshly pressed, or dry-cleaned robes of righteousness. If David had stood tall and strong and not given in to his fleshly desires, their whole lives could have been turned around. I guarantee if he had moved out, and stopped having sex with Sabrina, she would have made the right decision. If David had removed himself from her home, then she could have taken a long hard look at her life and decided whether or not she wanted to marry him. If she did, then a wedding could have been planned. I know it could have taken place much sooner than a year, but you see, fear, as well as flesh, entered the picture. They were not able to see clearly and correctly.

Can you imagine what it would be like for a groom to see his bride walking down the isle in filthy, dirty clothes? Her hair is a mess. Her face is all smeared with mud. The terrible odor that comes from her pores is so horrible that no one can stand to get near her. She isn't even wearing D.O. for her B.O. I guarantee if a man saw this filthy, stinky monster coming toward him to spend the rest of his life with, we wouldn't have the movie *"The Runaway Bride,"* instead it would be *"The Runaway Groom."* No man wants a woman who acts like a man, talks like a man, sweats like a man, or looks like a man. He wants a woman who is clean, pretty, soft, gentle...who brushes her hair and smells good. We women also want a man to be clean, well-groomed, wear nice cologne, and is also aware of his appearance.

33

Doing it Right!

Our son Shawn got married to a beautiful bride. She absolutely looked like an angel on their wedding day. Shawn was so excited to be getting married. Here he was, a 22-year-old, virgin, and God blessed him with someone so beautiful inwardly as well as outwardly. To give a bit of background: Shawn made a commitment at the age of 13. We gave him a covenant ring in front of the church body. He made a covenant with God, his parents, and the congregation that he would keep himself pure and holy until the night of his marriage. The covenant ring was worn on his left ring finger and would not be removed until the day of his wedding. It would then be replaced with his wedding band, thus making a new covenant with God and his new bride to stay married for life.

On the night of his wedding, my husband conducted the marriage ceremony. When it came time for the exchange of rings, Stan talked about Shawn's covenant ring and how he stayed pure. The ring had Ephesians 5:27 inscribed on the outside. Because of the inscription, this ring became a tremendous testimony over the years. Shawn was able to profess for many years, even to strangers, that he would stay pure until the day of his marriage. The whole congregation was very happy for Shawn and Rachel, because they all knew that they had kept their relationship pure and holy before God. I asked Shawn what he and Rachel did to keep the covenant with the Lord. He said, "Mom, it was really easy. We made a decision, and we stuck to that decision. We loved and respected each other not to sin. It was a lot easier than I ever thought possible."

If we are to be the Bride of Christ, then we need to think about our lives. Does the Lord see a beautiful, clean, righteous, holy bride coming towards Him, or, does He see that bride filthy inside and out?

Just imagine what this beautiful wedding dress is going to look like for the Bride of Christ. There are going to be many of us, His brides trying to fit in one gigantic, gorgeous, spectacular, fancy, glittering wedding

34

gown. When the time comes and we all step into this gown, we will be prepared and ready to meet our groom.

Remember, the Lord is looking for His bride to be without spot, wrinkle, or blemish, to be holy. Unfortunately people, we are far from having this dream opportunity. He is giving us grace right now to change, even as He is separates the wheat from the tares. Do you want to be separated from Jesus, or, do you want to make things right with Him?

Ephesians 5:27 *That he might present it to himself a glorious church, <u>not having spot, or wrinkle, or any such thing; but that it should be holy and without blemish.</u>*

Making it Right!

After several months went by, David and Sabrina made things right. They had our son Shawn, who is a pastor, marry them in the church. Hallelujah! The Lord is gracious. I pray that the following Scriptures convict your heart concerning these truths.

Mark 7:21 *For from within, out of the heart of men, proceed evil thoughts, adulteries, fornications, murders,*

Acts 15:29 *That ye <u>abstain from ... fornication:</u> from which if ye keep yourselves, ye shall do well. Fare ye well.*

1 Corinthians 5:9-11 *I wrote unto you in an epistle <u>not to company with fornicators:</u> Yet not altogether with the fornicators of this world, or with the*

35

covetous, or extortioners, or with idolaters; for then must ye needs go out of the world. But now I have written unto you not to keep company, if any man that is called a brother be a fornicator, or covetous, or an idolater, or a railer, or a drunkard, or an extortioner; with such an one no not to eat.

1 Corinthians 6:9 *Know ye not that the unrighteous shall not inherit the kingdom of God? Be not deceived: neither fornicators, nor idolaters, nor adulterers, nor effeminate, nor abusers of themselves with mankind,*

1 Corinthians 6:18 *Flee fornication. Every sin that a man doeth is without the body; but he that committeth fornication sinneth against his own body.*

1 Corinthians 7:2 *Nevertheless, to avoid fornication, let every man have his own wife, and let every woman have her own husband.*

2 Corinthians 12:21 *And lest, when I come again, my God will humble me among you, and that I shall bewail many which have sinned already, and have not repented of the uncleanness and fornication and lasciviousness which they have committed.*

Galatians 5:19-21 *Now the works of the flesh are manifest, which are these; Adultery, fornication, uncleanness, lasciviousness, Idolatry, witchcraft, hatred, variance, emulations, wrath, strife, seditions, heresies, Envyings, murders, drunkenness, revellings, and such like: of the which I tell you before, as I have also told you in time past, that they which do such things shall not inherit the kingdom of God.*

1 Thessalonians 4:3 For *this is the will of God, even your sanctification, that ye should abstain from fornication:*

1 Thessalonians 4:7 *For God hath not called us unto uncleanness, but unto holiness.*

Ungodly Soul Ties

What is an ungodly soul tie? An ungodly soul tie is created with whom we have had sexual intercourse or even engaged in heavy petting with. This includes oral and anal sex. It does not matter whether or not you had sexual arousal. If this has occurred with anyone outside of marriage, then you have created an ungodly soul tie with that person. Men and women, if you have had sexual fantasies about another person, you have an ungodly soul tie with them. When you commit the sin of masturbation because of watching a filthy film, looking at a magazine, fantasizing, etc., you have made an ungodly soul tie with the other person. What about abortion? If someone performs this despicable act against someone and takes the baby from the womb, you have created an ungodly soul tie with the person performing the procedure. Obviously any kind of molestation, sexual perversion, and sin against someone causes an ungodly soul tie. Even if the sin was committed against you, there is an ungodly soul tie that needs to be broken.

Why is it Important to Break this Tie?

The reason to break the tie is because when two people have sex, even if it involves mutual masterbation while the couple views a magazine or film, the two become one. Do not disregard an ungodly soul tie happening because of masturbation by looking at a magazine or film. You still become one with an ungodly soul tie attached to you. Just as married couples become one flesh the night of the consummation of their love, the same is true in the other scenarios listed previously. You take that person to bed with you each and every night until you break the tie. The sin has not been removed from your spirit until you take action to remove the sin in the Name of Jesus.

How do I Break this Filthy Tie?

First, renounce all sexual sins with another. Name the name of the person you had sexual encounters with out loud. If it was a film or show, speak it out and renounce the sin. Command the ungodly soul tie to be severed and broken. Command in the Name of Jesus that no longer will there be an ungodly soul tie bound to your body, soul, or spirit. Ask forgiveness of the Lord and also forgive those who may have harmed and hurt you. Declare that any ungodly soul ties from past generations be broken, severed, and removed from you from the very first thought, word, gesture, or deed. Command these ungodly soul ties to be severed from the tenth generation or as far back as need be. Pray also that the generations now and to come will be free from all ungodly soul ties in the Name of Jesus.

Just Do It!

In the book of John, Chapter Two, the Lord is speaking about marriage. The marriage of the Lord with the "Bride of Christ," refers to us. Jesus is calling His disciples to Him. He tells us to be servants and to "Just Do It." Since we are just pots of clay that are molded by our Lord, in John 2:7, the Lord says, "Fill the waterpots with water and fill them to the brim." Why would He say this? John the Baptist baptizes us in water for the remission of our sins. This baptism is a symbol or picture of accepting Jesus as our Lord and Savior. We are to be clean clear to the brim. Jesus then turned the water into wine. He will not fill an old wineskin with new wine. ***In other words, the Lord desires us to be clean all the way. Praise God, we have a loving, forgiving Lord who cleanses us from all unrighteousness!***

Remember, to receive a crown we must:

Ephesians 4:22-24 *That ye <u>put off</u> concerning the former conversation <u>the old man</u>, which is corrupt according to the deceitful lusts; And be renewed in the spirit of your mind; And that ye <u>put on the new man</u>, which after God is created in righteousness and true holiness.*

Crown of Glory

Chapter 4

I Don't Care, I Want to!

Psalms 66:18 *If I regard iniquity in my heart, the Lord will not hear me:*

The word abomination is ugly sounding. It means something disgusting, something the Lord loathes, dislikes very much and hates. According to the Word of God, there are abominations we do to ourselves, and there are abominations we commit against God. You might be thinking, "Well, I don't have to worry about committing an abomination against God or myself because I believe in the "New Testament". I don't have to worry about that "Old Testament". It is true that Galatians 3:13 it says,

Galatians 3:13 *Christ hath redeemed us from the curse of the law, being made a curse for us: for it is written, Cursed is every one that hangeth on a tree:*

41

However, does this Scripture do away with the law? Are you now free to commit sins such as; lying, stealing, adultery, and fornication? What this Scripture means is that Christ took away the curse of the law, but not the curse of the Lord. Jesus became the curse for us, and we now have His grace that results in our forgiveness. By having sins listed in the Old Testament, we can identify what sin is. We do not need the law for salvation and eternal life; however, the law does help identify what God dislikes and considers to be sin.

Struggling With Sin

Romans 7:7 *What shall we say then? Is the law sin? God forbid. Nay, I had not known sin, but by the law: for I had not known lust, except the law had said, Thou shalt not covet.*

Matthew 5:17 *Think not that I am come to destroy the law, or the prophets: I am not come to destroy, but to fulfill.*

The Scriptures of the Old Testament help us to see that the law is necessary to be a guide for every Christian to follow. In the New Testament, the Lord spoke of a new commandment we must keep. This commandment is that we love one another as He loves us. Think about the commandments of the Old Testament; namely, the Ten Commandments.

The Ten Commandments

1. The first commandment is to not have any other gods before Him.

2. The second commandment is to not make any graven image.

3. The third commandment is to not take the name of the Lord thy God in vain.

4. The fourth commandment is to remember and keep the Sabbath day holy.

5. The fifth commandment is to honor your father and mother.

6. The sixth commandment is to not kill.

7. The seventh commandment is to not commit adultery.

8. The eighth commandment is to not steal.

9. The ninth commandment is to not bear false witness against thy neighbor.

10. And, the last but of course not least, the tenth commandment is to not covet thy neighbor's house, etc.

If we will follow the new commandments Jesus gave, it pretty much covers the Ten Commandments in the Old Testament.

> **John 13:34-35** *__A new commandment I give unto you,__ __That ye love one another; as I have loved you, that__ __ye also love one another.__ By this shall all men know that ye are my disciples, if ye have love one to another.*

Abominations and Curses

The difference between an abomination and a curse is that a curse, according to *Webster's Dictionary* is an evil misfortune that comes as if in response to imprecation or as retribution. It is many times passed from one generation to the next. So, does that mean if the curse is passed on from one generation to the next, the sin involved is not my fault? To a certain extent, that is correct; however, we still have choices to make. With the Lord's help, we can be free from bondages passed from one generation to the next.

> **Exodus 34:7** *Keeping mercy for thousands, forgiving iniquity and transgression and sin, and __that will__ __by no means clear the guilty;__ visiting the iniquity of the fathers upon the children, and upon the children's children, unto the third and to the fourth generation.*

As we see in Scripture, the iniquity, transgression and sins are forgiven, but by no means are the guilty cleared. The Lord does allow blessings, as well as curses, to come our way.

44

Deuteronomy 11:26-28 *Behold, I set before you this day a blessing and a curse;* <u>*A blessing, if ye obey the commandments of the LORD your God, which I command you this day:*</u> *And a <u>curse, if ye will not obey the commandments of the LORD your God</u>, but turn aside out of the way which I command you this day, to go after other gods, which ye have not known.*

Abominations Unto Us, Violating Dietary Laws

A curse is not having the supernatural protection of God, and a blessing is being under His supernatural protection. Curses are passed down from one generation to the next in several areas—one is through the things we eat.

Leviticus 3:17 *It shall be a perpetual <u>statute</u> for your generations throughout all your dwellings, that ye eat neither fat nor blood.*

This statute or law is continual; it was never done away with. This statute contains an abomination to man as noted in Leviticus, Chapter 11, and Deuteronomy, Chapter 14; but, you say, "Leslie, we're told in the New Testament that all things were clean and okay to eat." When we break the law, we sin against our own bodies, because these laws were given to us for our own protection. As you read Leviticus, Chapter 11, you will note that 14 times it is mentioned that certain things we eat are clean. Also, it mentions things that are unclean and an abomination. Therefore, for our own protection and health we should avoid eating certain animals.

45

According to the Word of God, the unclean animals we should avoid eating for our own health includes: The camel, coney (a type of a rabbit), pig, and anything not having fins and scales (such as shrimp). We are not to eat the eagle, ossifrage, ospray, vulture, kite, raven, owl, night hawk, cuckow, cormorant (sea bird), swan, pelican, stork, heron, lapwing (shore inhabiting bird), bat, fowls that creep on all fours, and other flying or creeping things that have four feet. Also included are the weasel, mouse, tortoise, ferret, chameleon, lizard, snail, mole and other creeping crawling things. YUK! I do not know about you, but there are not too many of these unclean animals mentioned that I would really care to eat, much less try, even the poor little bunny rabbits, as well as that absolute most awful critter, the lizard. Why do we have to have those dreadful looking things on this planet anyway?

However, I love shrimp. I have a question for God. "Why do you say it's okay for us to eat the locust, beetle, and the grasshopper? I could dip them in chocolate and still not want to eat them! How can it be that something as yummy as shrimp be so bad for our bodies? It is so true that His ways are higher than ours and His thoughts are above ours. We just cannot make sense of the things of God, sometimes.

Isaiah 55:9 *For as the heavens are higher than the earth, so are my ways higher than your ways, and my thoughts than your thoughts.*

As you read the Scriptures in Leviticus and Deuteronomy, you will find something important to remember, that is, if we eat an unclean animal it will be an abomination to us, not to God. He simply informs us of things that are good and healthy for us and things that are bad or unhealthy for us. Does that mean I'll go to hell if I eat rabbit? Well, maybe if it's cute or a family pet. (Just kidding!) No, it simply means it is unclean for you, and it would be best for you, as a temple of the Holy Spirit, to not partake of these animals listed.

I Don't Care, I Want To!

Violating Sexual Laws

Another law that we violate to the detriment of our own bodies is covered in Leviticus Chapters 18 and 20, as well as 1 Corinthians 6:18.

1 Corinthians 6:18 *Flee fornication. Every sin that a man doeth is without the body; but he that committeth fornication sinneth against his own body.*

However, a real eye opener in the Scripture concerns what will happen to us if we violate our own bodies by partaking in these sexual sins.

1 Corinthians 3:16-17 *Know ye not that ye are the temple of God, and that the Spirit of God dwelleth in you? If any man defile the temple of God, him shall God destroy; for the temple of God is holy, which temple ye are.*

Romans 1:32 *Who knowing the judgment of God, that they which commit such things are worthy of death, not only do the same, but have pleasure in them that do them.*

Many of us believe that sexual sins are confined to homosexuality, fornication, and adultery. Let's not forget about those believers who commit a secret, hidden sin. Do you really think that you are getting away with anything if you masturbate? This is an abomination to our Lord. Men, if you are passing your seed, then you are still committing sex outside of marriage. You are stealing from your mate or future mate. The Lord said to be fruitful and multiply. There is no fruit in masturbation.

47

I would sure like for the leaders of the Church to start ministering to their congregations and speak forthrightly to them. Many men look for a woman who is a virgin to marry; yet they continue to masturbate and commit sin. Many times this same man will yet consider himself a virgin, if he hasn't had sex with a woman. Whether a man or woman masturbates, it is still involves sexual pleasure and you are stealing from your marriage partner, whether you are married or not. Older men, plead with your young men to not give into this temptation. You older men need to stop, also.

I praise the Lord that I have a bold husband in the Lord. He called a mandatory meeting for all men of the church, age 12 and up. All the men of the church, except one, showed up. He then had them secretly write down whether they have ever or are now masturbating. Out of all the men, only one said that he hadn't. In our congregation where we preach holiness and righteousness continuously, if that percentage have masturbated, or still are, think how many fall into this trap of the devil all across the globe.

Men and women, when this sin is committed in your marriage, you will cause a jealous spirit to come upon your spouse. If this is a difficult sin for you to get rid of, it could be a generational curse working in your life; however, you are still guilty. The husband or the wife may not even know why he/she has this jealous spirit, but it is very evident. *Some of the manifestations of a jealous spirit are hatred, anger, maliciousness, murder, and strife.* Are there any of these manifestations in your home? If you are engaging in this sin, repent and never turn back.

Leviticus 18:21 *And **thou shalt not let any of thy seed pass through the fire to Molech**, neither shalt thou profane the name of thy God: I am the LORD.*

Genesis 38:9-10 *And Onan knew that the seed should not be his; and it came to pass, when he went in unto his brother's wife, that he spilled it on the*

*ground, lest that he should give seed to his brother.
And the thing which he did displeased the LORD:
wherefore he slew him also.*

Remember, the Lord does not want us to open the door to a perverted spirit. The world teaches that masturbation is normal, and it is something that should be done. Satan is fooling us if we listen to him. He wants to put you in bondage to sin. If we, as Christians would realize the consequences of the sexual sins we commit not only against others, but ourselves, maybe we would make a decision to stop. The Lord is a God of grace and mercy, and He forgives.

Numbers 5:28-30 *And if the woman be not defiled, but be clean; then she shall be free, and shall conceive seed. <u>This is the law of jealousies, when a wife goeth aside to another instead of her husband, and is defiled; Or when the spirit of jealousy cometh upon him, and he be jealous over his wife, and shall set the woman before the LORD</u>, and the priest shall execute upon her all this law.*

1 Corinthians 7:4 *The wife hath not power of her own body, but the husband: and likewise also the husband hath not power of his own body, but the wife.*

Spiritual Adultery

There is another aspect of adultery we need to address – spiritual adultery. What is spiritual adultery? Ministers have a lot to juggle with the different aspects and requirements of ministry. They are to be the priest of their home, the spiritual leader of the church and or other ministries

49

they may have. Many times they are also married and a parent. I have seen different ministries with the leader's marriage ending in divorce, the children having drug problems, children's pregnancies outside of marriage, etc., etc. A whole host of things come against these ministers. The fundamental reason is, of course, when you are serving Jesus in a ministry position, I guarantee you attacks will come, and they won't let up. The second reason, and one I believe many do not want to look at, is spiritual adultery. An example of this would be a pastor overseeing his "flock". Let's suppose a woman needs ministry and takes a lot of the pastor's time and effort. His wife needs him to come home and take care of some of the "honey do's," but the pastor doesn't come home until late in the evening, night after night, because of counseling this other woman. If the husband doesn't make his wife feel secure and reassure her that he will be there for her when she needs him, a jealous spirit will come upon her. She begins to feel threatened in her position as a wife and will become a real nuisance and nag toward her husband. Because of this jealous spirit, envy, strife, and every evil work enters the home. A spirit of anger has found an open door and will hang around.

Even if a man or woman is not a minister, but your garden-variety work-aholic, this spirit of jealousy, with all the manifestations, will enter the home. One way to find out if this spirit is in your home is; are you happy when you leave work but once you get close to home you start getting edgy and even a little angry? By the time you finally arrive, your adrenaline is pumping and you're agitated. Once inside your home, you start picking out everything that is wrong. The house is too messy. The kids didn't do what you asked them to do. The sink has a constant leak, and it's driving you crazy. Have you allowed a jealous spirit to enter your home?

On the other hand, if a wife is very "spiritual", many times the husband will turn away from her. He will begin to ignore her and even begin to make sure she heads for the church every time the doors are open. The reason for this is because he feels threatened spiritually. He feels that he could never measure up to her level as a Christian and certainly could never be as close to God as she is.

The pastor who is ministering to another woman should never do so alone. My husband and I minister together if a woman of our church needs counseling. If a man needs counseling, I would never consider being alone with him. Also, it is okay to say "no." As a minister, it is okay to say, "I can't counsel with you tonight, my family and I have plans." Another suggestion to present this is to always have several husband and wife pastoral teams in your church who are trained and available.

Regarding the wife who has a husband that feels threatened by her "spirituality." (Oh, and by the way, the man will never admit to this feeling, but the truth is that he does feel threatened.) The sad part is that the wife of this man feels she is superior to him. (And by the way, she will never admit to this feeling of superiority either.) She doesn't respect his authority or reverence him. Of course, this doesn't apply to all couples like this. A woman in this position must honor her husband. Reverence him and encourage him in the things of the Lord. Even if you see him do a sweet thing for you or someone else, begin to affirm him and you will see him turn toward the Lord in a greater way.

However, many times the woman prays and prays for her husband to fully serve the Lord; then when he turns around and does so, she doesn't know what to do. After all the times of prayer, fasting, and then even more prayer, the wife finds herself in a position unfamiliar to her. She was the one in control. She was the one who was spiritually stronger. The wife has only one Godly option: Allow the man you married to be the head of the house and respect him.

Remember wives, our life is so much better with the Lord; our husband, our children, and everything we're involved in when we reverence our husbands. Find ways to respect him. Turn the negative incidents around for the glory of the Lord. Don't be a nag or nuisance. Be joyful, considerate, happy and respectful. You are only responsible for your actions. Allow God to change you, and then see the Lord begin to work on your husband. If you are the one always praying for God to change your husband, then change that prayer to, "Lord, change me.

Make me more Christ-like. Make me a good wife, and help me to reverence and respect my husband. Help him to see Jesus in me. I choose this day to be joyful, for I know that the joy of the Lord is my strength. In Jesus name. Amen."

Remember, you can only decide for yourself whether to be happy or not. It is not up to anyone else to do this for you.

Ephesians 5:33 *Nevertheless let every one of you in particular so love his wife even as himself; and the wife see that she reverence her husband.*

Chapter 5

Sins of Sodomy

1 King 15:11-12 *And Asa did that which was right in the eyes of the LORD, as did David his father. And he took away the sodomites out of the land, and removed all the idols that his fathers had made.*

As Christians we think that sodomy only applies to homosexuals. According to *Webster's Dictionary,* sodomy is copulation with a member of the same sex or with an animal. Also, sodomy is unnatural copulation with a member of the opposite sex. An unnatural copulation with a member of the opposite sex includes anal and oral sex. The sins of sodomy include incest, adultery, masturbation, homosexuality, bestiality, abortion, and last, but not to be omitted, sexual intercourse with a female during her menstrual cycle.

A woman in her cycle is actually more prone to infection during this time. I believe the Lord included a Scripture to abstain from having sexual intercourse with a woman during this menstrual cycle as a protection for the female. I know that for the most part, women today keep themselves cleaner and healthier than they were able to in biblical times. However, there is still medical proof that the time of a woman's period, she is more vulnerable to infection. For example, if the husband has a cold during that time, the wife is more likely to get the infection as well. Husbands, if you love your wife as Christ loves the church, then why would you put your beautiful bride in harm's way? The time of prohibiting sexual intercourse according to the Word of God, is seven days. It's okay, you super stud men, you can make it! Do not go and sin by masturbating during that time. Stay in the Word of God and get closer to the Lord!

> **Leviticus 20:18** *And if a man shall lie with a woman having her sickness, and shall uncover her nakedness; he hath discovered her fountain, and she hath uncovered the fountain of her blood: and both of them shall be cut off from among their people.*

> **Leviticus 15:24** *And if any man lie with her at all, and her flowers be upon him, he shall be unclean seven days; and all the bed whereon he lieth shall be unclean.*

> **Leviticus 15:28** *But if she be cleansed of her issue, then she shall number to herself seven days, and after that she shall be clean.*

Now that we got all of those "**M**" words, (masturbation and menstruation) out of the way, the good news is that we can repent and turn away from such sin. Our Lord will make us righteous once again. Do not receive or allow a spirit of condemnation to come on you regarding these things. Realize the Lord could be convicting you, and He wants you to make it right with Him. Ask the Lord for a fresh new start, and He will bless you. Help your children; stay strong in the Lord, by teaching them while they are young and at home the truth of God's Word. By God's grace, they won't fall into these snares of the devil.

> **Ephesians 5:3** *But fornication, and all uncleanness, or covetousness, let it not be once named among you, as becometh saints;*

> **Ephesians 5:6-10** *Let no man deceive you with vain words: for because of these things cometh the wrath of God upon the children of disobedience. Be not ye therefore partakers with them. For ye were sometimes darkness, but now are ye light in the Lord: walk as children of light: (For the fruit of the Spirit is in all goodness and righteousness and truth;) Proving what is acceptable unto the Lord.*

> **Ephesians 5:17** *Wherefore be ye not unwise, but understanding what the will of the Lord is.*

> **Ephesians 5:20-21** *Giving thanks always for all things unto God and the Father in the name of our Lord Jesus Christ; Submitting yourselves one to another in the fear of God.*

Marriage Bed Is Undefiled

As Christians, we need to be careful as to what we think is appropriate in everything we do. Christian married couples, many of you justify your ungodly actions by quoting where it says, in Hebrews 13:4, the marriage bed is *undefiled*. Therefore, we can indulge ourselves whatever sexual pleasures we want to. Think about that statement. What do the homosexuals, whether male or female do for sexual pleasure? Sexual gratification comes to them two ways. One is oral sex and the other is anal sex. If Jesus is in your bedroom, oh, and by the way, He is, would He be happy to see how you, as husband and wife make love to each other? In Leviticus, Chapter 18 and Romans 1:26-27, we are instructed to abstain from these sort of sexual pleasures. They are abominations to our Lord.

> **Romans 1:26-27** *For this cause God gave them up unto vile affections: for even their <u>women did change the natural use into that which is against nature:</u> And likewise also the <u>men, leaving the natural use of the woman,</u> burned in their lust one toward another; men with men working that which is unseemly, and receiving in themselves that recompense of their error which was meet.*

The definition of defile, according to *Webster's Dictionary,* means to make unclean or impure. This word also means to corrupt the purity or perfection of someone or something and to make physically unclean, especially with something unpleasant or contaminating. Defilement is a dishonor. Obviously, the opposite of defile is to be undefiled. In other words keep holy, clean and pure. To not defile would be to not contaminate. What about oral sex? Is it clean? Is it holy? Is this the way God intended for married couples to be pleased sexually?

> **Romans 1:20** *For the invisible things of him from the creation of the world are clearly seen, being understood by the things that are made, even his eternal power and Godhead; so that they are without excuse:*

Romans 1:24 *Wherefore God also gave them up to uncleanness through the lusts of their own hearts, to dishonor their own bodies between themselves:*

I don't have proof about the following, but it makes sense to me. People get cold sores on their mouth or inside their mouth, sometimes called canker sores. This virus is actually Herpes. If someone with Herpes on or in the mouth has oral sex with someone, then they contaminate him or her in their private parts. This is why I believe that at least sometimes Herpes is present, even when the couple has been faithful to each other. I have heard of cases where both the husband and wife have only been with their marriage partner and sometimes sores appear. Not long ago I was ministering to a woman at *The Perfect Touch Women's Conference*. She made the statement to me that she has only had sex with her husband and vise versa. Nevertheless, they were struggling with sores that continue to appear. I ministered to her about what the Lord says about oral sex and she repented. The Lord is gracious and ever so forgiving. I have also heard reports of chronic sore throats and infections that can't be cleared up by antibiotics.

A recent survey that I heard about involved interviews with high school students. Ninety percent of the students admitted to having had oral sex. The reason they gave was because they felt they were safe from unwanted pregnancies and diseases. What these young people don't realize is that if someone has a sexually transmitted disease it can also be passed on to them through oral sex.

I want to please my Lord in all. I know He watches every move I make, all intents of my heart, and nothing is hidden from Jesus about me. There are God-given natural sexual pleasures given to man and there are unnatural, ungodly pleasures that not only the world and sinners commit, but Christians as well. We need to wake up and see just what sins we are committing against our Lord. Remember, you will have an ungodly soul tie with the person, whether through oral sex, anal sex, or intercourse.

Whenever I have spoken on this issue, it is amazing to me how many men or women come to me and say, "I don't know if I will find pleasure and satisfaction without oral sex." Some say, "I really have found that I enjoy anal sex or oral sex and it is very pleasing to me." Then as I begin to teach about these being abominations to the Lord, they want to get free. They realize that Satan has a grip on them. He has them bound and believing a lie. Satan has them involved in perversion. Once they realize this, they want to be free. When there is sin in the bedroom, it will cause many arguments to arise, also hatred, envy, strife, and every evil work. If your marriage bed is suffering, study the Scripture and find the truth for your own life and heart. Being cleansed is a daily process. We must continue learning the truth and staying teachable.

I know that these words of truth aren't pleasing to many of you right now; however, I believe that is why God wanted me to write this book. I am not afraid of telling it like it is. Sin is sin whether you are a believer in the Lord Jesus Christ or a sinful person of the world on your way to hell. Sodomy is sodomy no matter who commits it. If a man or woman freely makes the choice to be a sodomite, then both will have to answer to God for their actions.

God Reveals Sin

On a Saturday afternoon, I laid down to take a short nap. As I was sitting on the bed praying as I always do before going off to sleep, I asked the Lord to speak to me about whatever He would like. I prayed that if He had a dream or a vision for me or wanted to show me an area of my life I needed to change to let me know. As I began to lay my head upon my pillow, I had a vision. This was a vision where the whole room disappeared, and all I saw was the vision. The vision the Lord showed me was like an atomic bomb—a huge explosion. I didn't hear any noise I only saw the explosion. In this billow of smoke, I saw a face. The explosion and face were shown to me from the ground up. As the vision focused on the bigger mushroom part of the smoke, the face became very clear. Imagine a horror film where a killer has placed a plastic wrap around the victim, and the victim is suffocating. The eyes are wide open with fear and are protruding. The victim's mouth is open with looks of gasping for air. This is what the face looked like in the smoke from the bomb.

As you can imagine, I shot right up in bed and began to pray. I asked, "Lord, what are you trying to tell me? Is there something you are telling me or I need to tell others about? Please speak to me." I went ahead and laid back down and actually fell right to sleep.

I had a dream. In this dream, many of our congregation's members and others that I did not know, were present. The people were straddling a fence. Some were leaning to the right and others to the left. I then began to see different ones of our small congregation committing different kinds of sin. I saw myself speaking to them and confronting their sins. I told them to not straddle the fence anymore. They needed to make a decision. The Lord is tired of us going from one side to the other. Either our desire is to try and walk a righteous path or we choose the side of our flesh and Satan. We need to make a decision.

The next moment I heard the Lord speak so LOUDLY that I sat straight up and bed and began to shake. The Lord said, "TELL MY PEOPLE TO **WAKE UP!**" I was so startled and shaken that all I could do was pray. Having the anointing and gifts of a prophet is not always fun. I surely don't want to know the people's sins. I most assuredly don't enjoy confronting them. I knew that the next morning during the church service, I was going to have to say some difficult things to the people I love so much in our church.

That evening we had a function at the church. As I was driving to church, I had tears running down my face and was crying out to God. "We, your people have done such evil." My heart felt like it was being ripped open. I called out to the Lord and asked, "Is there anything else, Lord?" With that He showed me the names of four cities. The first was

Dallas, Texas. The second was West Palm Beach, Florida. The third was New Orleans, Louisiana, and the fourth was St. Louis, Missouri. I inquired, "Lord what about these cities? Are they connected with the vision of the bomb exploding? What about them?" Very clearly I heard the Lord speak in that still, small voice.

He said, "My children in Dallas and West Palm Beach think they are high and mighty in the Kingdom of God. There is a haughty spirit over them that is keeping them from righteousness. In New Orleans, there is corruption in the high places of My churches. The church leaders have committed sexual sins and have disgraced Me from the pulpit. St. Louis will be an example for My people, which side are they going to choose? Right now My children are riding the fence. One foot in evil, the other in holiness."

I saw the picture in my mind of the Arch. The Arch was destroyed, stating that it was an example of an idol to many. He wants us to make the ultimate decision to follow Him.

When I got to church, I was still feeling pretty shaky. The Lord showed me there was molestation and incest from the past that had not been dealt with in one of our church families. I went up to one of the daughters of this family who was 13. I asked her if she had been molested or hurt by someone in the family. She mentioned that her older brother had molested her. The events that transpired within that family after that were astonishing, another sin issue was cursing with their mouth. The family began to cry out to the Lord for healing and direction.

When molestation or any other sexual perversion takes place in someone's life, whether they are the perpetrator or the victim, the door is opened for the formation of ungodly soul ties. The curse is passed from generation to generation. Many people who have been sexually violated as a child either turn around and become a perpetrator, become a homosexual, or their children have the same thing happen to them. We need to take authority in the name of Jesus over these sexual perversions from past generations. Sever the ungodly soul ties and pray daily until you know the curse is gone. *(See Chapter 3, page 38.)*

Other areas of sin present in our congregation and the Body of Christ at large that the Lord revealed to me involved anal sex, pornography, masturbation, and other sexual perversions. After mentioning these sins to our congregation, the floodgates opened and filth was revealed. I was surprised. Many began to repent and ask forgiveness. A true cleansing began to take place since these sins that were revealed pertained not only to our congregation, but also to all of the Lord's children. The Lord was revealing what many believers need to repent of.

I asked the Lord, "Why do you reveal so many sins to our congregation and the leaders of our church?" Then it dawned on me that probably 80 percent of the congregation is constantly asking the Lord to forgive them. They ask the Lord to cleanse them, and make them holy and righteous. We ask regularly, "Lord if there is any sin in our lives, forgive us and cleanse us from all unrighteousness." The Lord is faithful to answer those prayers, but sometimes it's painful to make the changes we need to make for righteousness' sake.

Don't forget that we have a forgiving Father who loves us very much. He desires that we become cleansed.

Remember, to be free from abominations unto ourselves and to our Lord, we need to be truthful with ourselves and not let our hearts deceive us in any way.

Jeremiah 17:9-10 *The <u>heart is deceitful above all</u>*

things, and desperately wicked: who can know it? I the LORD search the heart, I try the reins, even to give every man according to his ways, and according to the fruit of his doings.

Chapter 6

Crown of Thorns

John 19:2 *And the soldiers platted a <u>crown of thorns</u>, and put it on his head, and they put on him a purple robe,*

To understand what it really means to receive a crown from the Lord, we need to first comprehend what Jesus Christ went through for us. A crown of thorns was placed on Jesus' head for us, His children.

Not long ago, I had a vision of this perfect, beautiful red rose. The rose was just in between being a bud and in full bloom. The rose stem still had the thorns protruding from it; however, there was such a sweet aroma coming from this one flower. As I and others were smelling its sweet aroma, the thorns began to fall off one by one. The Lord then spoke to me and said, "My people are like this beautiful rose to me. I will cast out to them a beautiful fragrance, enough to fill a room. Also, as I hand each of them a beautiful rose, I will remove the thorns from the stem so that My children won't be pricked by the thorn. I took the pain of the thorns pricking one so that My sons and daughters would not have to endure the pain. I will take them from being like a young innocent bud to a flower in full bloom. Next I saw the thorns on my Savior's head. The Lord loves us so much that he was willing to go through such torment and pain for us. Yes, you and me. He is no respecter of persons.

Thorns Hurt

The crown of thorns the soldiers placed on Jesus head was to mock and make fun of Him. As I was thinking about what my Lord went through for me, He reminded me of an event that occurred in my life. I used to live in Odessa, Texas, which is in West Texas. For those of you who don't know what a grass burr, or "sticker" as I used to call them is, those little cactus-like weeds could hurt! I remember once when I was a child riding my bike in a "cleared", open field next to our house. I knew that I was being disobedient and I was not supposed to go that way home, but I decided to take a shortcut. I almost made it home when, unfortunately, I hit a good-sized rock and fell off my bike. The most awful part about it was that I landed right in the middle of a "sticker contest". There was a big patch of them in this "cleared field", and I just happened to find the one spot where a bunch of them were. Oh, how my backside wanted to be somewhere else. As you can imagine, I had a hard time walking the rest of the way home, because my whole back and rump were full of those nasty things. I still cringe today when I think about the pain those grass burrs caused me. Then I think of Jesus. He had the crown of thorns placed on His head for me. These were not small thorns, and they were much bigger than the tiny thorns I grew up with in West Texas.

Another time in Phoenix, Arizona, when I was eight years old; my dad, older sister Robin, and I had climbed up a mountain, and on the way down

I stepped on a small cactus. I was crying because it hurt so much when Robin, my older sister, said, "Sit down, I cleared a spot for you." "Yeah right!" No sooner did I hit the ground that I felt an enormous pain in my "buckets". Not only did I have a cactus stuck to my rump, but also I had one on my foot. My dad had to pick me up and carry me down the mountain. The point is that thorns, no matter how big or small, are always painful. Our daddy God is there to pick us up and carry us away from the pain. My dad had to physically remove each thorn, one by one. This is what our Lord does for us as well. He removes the bruises and wounds in our hearts, one by one.

Did you ever get a cut on your head somewhere? If so, do you remember how much blood there was? When my son Shawn was three years old, he jumped on his grandma's bed and hit the headboard. He hit the worst spot, because there was a point protruding out of it, and when he sat up there was a cut in the middle of his forehead. It scared me so much, not because the cut looked so bad, but because of all the blood that poured from his forehead. As a young mom, I remember having thoughts like, "Oh no, he's going to bleed to death!" I was all ready for bed, pajamas and all. I knew I was going to have to take him to the hospital and get the cut sewn up. Blood was everywhere, all over the sheets, the headboard, and me. In my state of confusion, all common sense fled for the moment. I wasn't even going to take the time to change from my pj's into clothing. The blood scared me, and I was going to head to the hospital in my pj's right then. That was how scared this small cut on my child's head made me. Fortunately, my mother-in-law was with me, and she helped calm me down. Yes, I put some clothes on before I took Shawn to the hospital.

As I was pondering about Jesus wearing the crown of thorns for us, I remember my child and the amount of blood coming from his head. I realized that Jesus must not only have been in severe pain, but He must have been covered in blood. Christ went to His death in its most terrifying, vile form to bear all our sins. Jesus put on the crown of thorns, just to demonstrate His great love for us. Yes, you and me. We, as sinful human beings, were the ones who deserved this kind of punishment, yet Jesus took and wore this painful crown. Instead, the Lord gives us the ability to wear the crown of glory, which He deserved. Jesus committed no sin, yet he submitted to a death with great shame and suffering all for us.

> **Matthew 27:29** *And when they had platted a <u>crown of thorns</u>, they put it upon his head, and a reed in his right hand: and they bowed the knee before him, and mocked him, saying, Hail, King of the Jews!*

> **Mark 15:17** *And they clothed him with purple, and platted a <u>crown of thorns</u>, and put it about his head,*

> **John 19:2** *And the soldiers platted a <u>crown of thorns</u>, and put it on his head, and they put on him a purple robe,*

> **John 19:5** *Then came Jesus forth, wearing the <u>crown of thorns</u>, and the purple robe. And Pilate saith unto them, Behold the man!*

I want you to get the picture of this story of Jesus' trial and execution. The soldiers led Jesus away to their barracks. They struck Him with a rod or staff, spit on him in hateful mockery, fell down and "worshipped" Him. I can just see soldier after soldier perpetrating this violent crime upon our Savior, our Lord, our King. When they mocked Him, they took off the purple robe of royalty and put on His own clothes. Again, a mockery of our King, a *gorgeous* purple robe symbolizing royalty is what should have been placed on our Lord, with great reverence.

After this, the Lord carried His own cross and then the Roman soldiers compelled Simon of Cyrene, who was just passing by, to carry the Lord's cross. I sometimes think about what it would be like to be in Simon's place at that moment. He had to be frightened. Can you imagine the shock and disbelief that something like this was really happening to the Son of God? We do not always understand the ways of the Father. They are a mystery to us sometimes.

The Scriptures mention that the soldiers then attempted to give Jesus a drink of wine, mingled with myrrh, but the Lord refused it. Have you ever thought about why would He refuse the wine? Was it because the enemy was handing it to Him? Was it because He thought there was poison in the cup? Why would the Lord refuse the wine?

We have recently been introduced to many different types of essential pure oils: Like myrrh, frankincense, hyssop and rosemary, to mention a few. There are specific ailments in our bodies that natural oils help heal. Myrrh, for example, is like an analgesic. It is a calming oil, an oil that allows the pain to cease.

Mark 15:23 *And they gave him to drink <u>wine mingled with myrrh: but he received it not</u>.*

I believe the reason Jesus refused this drink of wine with myrrh was He did not want any of His senses to be numbed. He wanted to be totally aware of everything that was going on. The Father sent Jesus with a prophetic mission, and He was destined to complete it. The herb myrrh in the days of Christ, was a drug given to those who were about to be crucified. The myrrh was mingled in with wine and was served to the prisoners to deaden the horrendous agony of crucifixion. However, our Lord Jesus wanted to bear all of our sins, pain, and transgressions in their totality.

Our Lord, Jesus Christ, was crucified for us. The word crucify according to the *Webster's Dictionary* means to put to death by nailing or binding to a cross and leaving the person to die of suffocation. Obviously, this is a very cruel and tormenting death, and Jesus endured this humiliating form of punishment for us. The Lord was exposed to our sin, as well as sickness and disease. Not only that, but He became like myrrh to us. When we have pain, sickness and disease the Lord removes them from us. He heals our emotions as well. Whatever area of your life that is painful for you was dealt with at the cross. He is there, pouring out His myrrh to us. If He had taken that drink, He would be just like all the other criminals; however, Jesus had a purpose and divine call from His Father to fulfill on our behalf.

Before the soldiers crucified our Lord, they tore up His clothing and cast lots for them. Here these soldiers were, practically flipping a coin to see who won His clothing. They mocked Him relentlessly by gambling for His clothing. Not once did they reverence Him, and they certainly didn't acknowledge Him as King. Satan still uses the same tactics today when mocking our King. The enemy comes in with counterfeit signs and wonders and tries to discredit the works of the Lord. To combat this, we must stand firmly on the promises of God. Stay sure-footed so that the enemy will not make you fall off that promise. The Scriptures tell us, when we have done all, stand.

Ephesians 6:13 *Wherefore take unto you the whole armour of God, that ye may be able to withstand in the evil day, and having done all, to stand.*

Those who have been in the military probably had the experience of having to stand there with someone yelling at you, with spit flying out of their mouth that landed on your face. Yet, you were courageous, obedient, and didn't move. As we resist the devil, he will flee. This is one of the greatest truths of our faith. You stand firmly long enough and the devil will get tired of harassing you and leave. He will probably find another area to tempt you in, but you learn to continually clean your life up and stand on the Word of God.

As the story continues of Jesus' crucifixion, prophecy would have to be fulfilled. It was at about 9:00 am, the third hour when the soldiers tormented, tortured, and crucified our Lord. The civil and religious leaders of the land searched for reasons to find Him guilty and kill Him. What accusations were they going to make to justify the Lord's crucifixion? Would it be because this man called Himself the Son of God? What about Him saying, "I am the God of Abraham, Isaac, and Jacob?" What about when Jesus stated that He was the God of the living not the dead? On a sign nailed to the top of the cross was the inscription accusing Him of only one thing. "The King of the Jews." All Jesus' statements were true, and no one could find fault with Him or His actions. People were healed, set free, delivered, and raised from the dead. Jesus further fulfilled prophecy as they crucified Him between two thieves. He was numbered with the transgressors.

> **Isaiah 53:12** *Therefore will I divide him a portion with the great, and he shall divide the spoil with the strong; because he hath poured out his soul unto death: and <u>he was numbered with the transgressors;</u> and he bare the sin of many, and made intercession for the transgressors.*

> **Mark 15:28** *And the Scripture was fulfilled, which saith, <u>AND HE WAS NUMBERED WITH THE TRANSGRESSORS.</u>*

As soldiers and others passed by, they blasphemed Him and shook their heads in disapproval. They mocked Him saying, "Save thyself, come down from the cross." You see, all these soldiers and witnesses of the crucifixion didn't understand that Jesus was saving all who would believe in Him, and that He would raise from the dead. Jesus is the one and only living God. He became our Savior, our Lord and King. You see, the Lord's greatest agony at that time was not His physical pain, but rather the pain and agony of lost souls since He bore the entire weight of the world's sin at that time. Jesus Christ became "sin for us".

69

2 Corinthians 5:221 *For he hath made him to be sin for us, who knew no sin; that we might be made the righteousness of God in him.*

The heavenly Father, the Holy God, cannot look with favor upon sin; therefore, He had to turn His face away from Jesus His Son. In reality, He let Jesus be a sacrificial lamb for us sinners. Do you ever feel that Jesus has turned His face away from you? Maybe you need to turn around. He is facing you...looking right at you.

Jesus allowed a crown of thorns to be placed on His head. In reality, what should have been placed on His head was a beautiful crown of gold. When someone in biblical days, as well presently, received a crown of gold, it was given to him/her with great honor and reverence. In the Word there are 13 references to a crown of gold. Our Jesus should have been crowned with a crown of gold! Instead, He received a crown of thorns when they mocked and whipped Him. He wore this crown of thorns, which was sharp and painful, so that a crown of gold can be placed on our heads. Jesus Christ is our great High Priest. We, the children of God, also become spiritual priests. Desire for your spiritual clothing to be clean to pursue righteousness so that a crown of gold can be placed on your head.

Remember, a beautiful crown of gold is given to us. We don't have to wear a painful,

ugly crown of thorns.

Psalms 21:3-4 *For thou preventest him with the blessings of goodness: thou settest a crown of pure gold on his head. He asked life of thee, and thou gavest it him, even length of days for ever and ever.*

71

Crown of Glory

Chapter 7

Crown of Anointing Oil

Leviticus 21:12 *Neither shall he go out of the sanctuary, nor profane the sanctuary of his God; for the <u>crown of the anointing oil of his God is upon him</u>: I am the LORD.*

In the Scriptures, there are 84 verses mentioning crowns. Many times the crowns were of pure gold. When I was slain in the spirit, the crown the Lord showed me was a beautiful, shiny, very glossy gold one with different colored jewels embedded in it. (See Chapter One) If we are to receive the crown of anointing oil of God, we need to stay pure and holy. We are not to depart from the faith and certainly not profane the Lords house. When we continue to do the Lord's will in our lives, He will anoint us with His anointing oil.

73

According to *Webster's Dictionary,* anoint means to rub oil or ointment on. An example is to put oil on in a ceremony of consecration. To consecrate means to set apart as holy. If we desire to be anointed, then we are to devote ourselves entirely and dedicate our life to the Lord.

Exodus 29:7 *Then shalt thou take the anointing oil, and pour it upon his head, and anoint him.*

When you are anointed with oil, it is also a symbol of washing away the old and bringing in the new. It is a symbol of the blood of Jesus washing you clean. It also represents healing, restoration, and renewal. When someone receives the crown of anointing oil, it is placing an anointing on you to hold the office of one of the Lord's fivefold ministries. He made some Apostles, some Prophets, some Evangelists, some Pastors and some Teachers.

The Apostle has the vision, the plan, and the desire to see the vision fulfilled no matter what the cost. The Prophet speaks out that the will of God might be fulfilled. This is the utmost desire of prophets. They see only black and white, what is true and false. The desire of a prophet is to let people know what is right and what is wrong in their lives according to His plan and word. **There is no gray area with a prophet!** You must be on the right side of the fence, or they will let you know. AMEN!

The desire of an Evangelist is to see lost souls come into the kingdom of God. Pastors in the fivefold ministry are the ones with loving hearts. They want to make sure that if anyone is hurting, they are comforted. Their desire is over the sheep. Teachers are the ones who study and know the Word backwards and forwards. They desire that the Word of God be taught accurately. They make sure that whoever is preaching or teaching is on target. The teacher will let the preacher know if they misquoted a Scripture or if they gave the wrong reference.

According to the Word of God, a pastor is not necessarily the one supposed to be leading the church. Apostles set up churches. Sometimes pastors are really apostles in charge of their church. Unfortunately, especially in this country, some preachers are anointed more as a teacher than pastors. Some preachers are evangelistic. The apostles always oversee. They are not always liked and many balk at seeing to it that the vision that the apostle has is fulfilled.

The prophet would not make a good church leader because they are not always appreciated nor liked. They will tell you just exactly what is going on, whether you like it or not! However, pastors aren't actually the best church leaders either. They usually have soft hearts and won't offend anyone even if it is needed. Unfortunately, our churches in America are in terrible condition when it comes to preaching the truth of God's Word. Over the years, we have lost the fivefold anointing in the churches. In every church, there should be an *apostle, prophet, pastor or pastors, teachers, and evangelists.* It is according to God's perfect plan that we, the Body of Christ, all come together in one place. If part of the body is missing (especially people of the fivefold ministry) then the ministry available is incomplete.

The Fivefold Offices

Apostle: **Has the Vision and desires for it to be fulfilled.**

Prophet: **Number one priority is the perfect will of God being realized.**

Evangelist: **Desires for the lost souls to be won into the Kingdom of God.**

Teacher: **Accurate teaching of the Word of God is most important.**

Pastor: **The well-being and stability of the sheep are their main concern.**

There are certain requirements we must fulfill to receive the crown of anointing oil. If we as righteous men/women and priests of the kingdom of God are to be joint heirs of Christ, then what are some of the requirements of priesthood as it relates to fivefold ministers?

Requirements to be a Priest

1   We shall not defile our bodies, nor others.

2   Men should not take a wife who won't repent of sexual sin or poor character.

3   When the Word says ...*he shall not go out of the sanctuary, nor profane the sanctuary*, we would say this refers to remaining strong in our faith and not cursing other believers.

4   Men should take a wife who is a virgin. I truly believe that even if we have sinned and engaged in premarital sex, if we now have repented the Lord can restore a spirit of virginity for us. Thank the Lord for His grace and mercy.

5   A man is not to profane his seed, which means he must not masturbate.

6   As blemishes are not permitted, this refers to being righteous and holy before our Lord.

These requirements are difficult to fulfill even when we earnestly desire to receive the crown of anointing oil. This spiritual crown is to be won now; we don't have to wait for eternal life to receive it. *I do not believe the fivefold ministry is for everyone;* however, I know the Lord anoints His own. In Psalm 28:8 it says, *"The Lord is the saving strength of his anointed."* In 2 Corinthians 1:21 it says, *"...he which stablisheth us has anointed us."* Verse 22, *...he hath sealed us.*

As believers we are to anoint with oil and cast out devils, anoint the sick and see them healed. Jesus was, and is, our example of how to pray for each other. He anointed the eyes of a blind man, and the man received sight. In James 5:14, the elders of the church are to pray over the sick, anoint them with oil in the Name of the Lord, and that the prayer of faith will save the sick.

How do you make anointing oil? Take virgin olive oil and add spices, or pure oils, for a sweet incense.

Exodus 30:25 *And thou shalt make it an oil of holy ointment, an ointment compound after the art of the apothecary: it shall be an holy anointing oil.*

Exodus 35:8 *And oil for the light, and spices for anointing oil, and for the sweet incense,*

Since Jesus is our crown of anointing oil, He is our protector. A prophetic act and declaration for you is to anoint the doors of your home, work place, vehicle, church, etc. Also, don't forget to anoint each other. Exodus 40 speaks of taking the anointing oil and sanctifying the altar, the tabernacle (the building), and the vessels (you and me), and they shall be holy.

Several places in the Word of God it mentions to not touch the Lord's anointed and to do His prophets no harm. Many times, as Christians we do evil things to each other. We end up hurting each other more than Satan and his demons ever could. We need to recognize that we should unite, not being divided in strife. We have a common purpose, a

77

common goal. This purpose is telling the world about our Lord Jesus Christ. Instead, we find something we don't like about another believer or minister and try and strip them of their anointing. Ministers are not perfect, and neither are you...not a one of us is. We do, however, have choices to make and need to make a vow before our Lord that we will strive to live a righteous, holy life. It isn't easy, but the Lord loves righteous men and hates wickedness.

When we receive His crown of anointing oil, then the Spirit of God comes upon us and He will anoint us to preach good tidings to the meek, heal the brokenhearted, and proclaim liberty to the captives, and the opening of prison doors to them who are bound.

The Year of the LORD's Favor

Isaiah 61:1 *The Spirit of the Lord GOD is upon me; because the <u>LORD hath anointed me to preach good tidings unto the meek; he hath sent us to bind up the brokenhearted, to proclaim liberty to the captives, and the opening of the prison</u> to them that are bound;*

This is truly the year of the Lord's favor. It can be for each of us if we strive and determine to be virtuous. Virtuous simply means having good moral character. If there be any virtue in you, (one that has general moral excellence, right action and thinking, goodness or morality, with effective power and ability to heal or strengthen), then think on the good things of the Lord.

Philippians 4:8 *Finally, brethren, whatsoever things are true, whatsoever things are honest, whatsoever things are just, whatsoever things are pure, whatsoever things are lovely, whatsoever things are*

*of good report; if there be any virtue, and if there
be any praise, think on these things.*

The Word of God tells us to not be unequally yoked. In other words, according to Scripture we aren't to associate with nonbelievers. We are also not to invite those who do not believe the doctrines of Jesus Christ into our home. If we do, then we are partakers of their evil deeds. To go one step further, according to the Word of God, if you conform to the world and the corruption of the world rather than lose a friend because they will **not** come out of the darkness, then you are an enemy of God. We are not to participate in the unfruitful works of darkness but are to expose them. With these truth in mind, are we to embrace a Mormon, Jehovah Witness, Hindu, Moslem, Buddhist, just to mention a few? I realize there are some nice friendly people in those religions. However, if we are going to be a disciple of the Most High God, our Jesus, Lord and Savior, then we need to decide which side of the fence we are going to sit. Years ago, I met some nice people within the world of the occult. However, according to the Word of God, I'm not to be friends with them or participate in activities with them.

Jehovah's Witnesses and Mormons are known to go door to door in their attempts to convert others. I have heard people say they will let them in to their home to "try and convince them they are wrong." How does this concept line up with Scripture? They do not believe in the same Jesus we believe in. Jehovah's Witnesses believe that Jesus is Michael, the Archangel. Mormons believe that Jesus was the brother of Lucifer. Just because someone says they believe in Jesus, it isn't necessarily the one true God they are talking about. We need to pray we will not be deceived.

**2 John 1:9 -11 *Whosoever transgresseth, and abideth
not in the doctrine of Christ, hath not God. He that
abideth in the doctrine of Christ, he hath both the
Father and the Son. If there come any unto you, and
bring not this doctrine, receive him not into your***

79

*house, neither bid him God speed: For he that
biddeth him God speed is partaker of his evil deeds.*

What about the god Allah? It is amazing how many Christians believe that this is the same Father God we serve. Does it make sense to you
that Jehovah God, He who considers being believers in Jesus Christ is Lord,
is the same god as the Moslems worship? This god, Allah, speaks through
the Koran and teaches the Moslems that they will go to Paradise for being
a martyr and killing Christians and Jews. Recognizing and comprehend-
ing this kind of evil is so far from our thinking that we can't even conceive
that people would embrace these beliefs.

When a religion, a nation, a person, a committee, a government, a
family, a ministry, etc. is under the control of Satan, this results in evil in
high places and the dominion of principalities of darkness. There is evil
around us that is so awful that most of us are in denial of its very exist-
ence. To our misfortune people, it is real. We need to wake up and stop
living by the naive adage that "nothing bad is going to happen to my
family or myself," and get on our faces and pray. You are **not** going to be
raptured out of this mess. Many of you will stray from your lifelong faith
in Jesus Christ, if you continue to believe you will just be swept off this
earth before anything evil happens. As you study, and I mean truthfully
study for yourself, and stay teachable as the Lord takes you through His
Word, you will find I am telling the truth. Many just listen to Endtimes
teachers and never study the Word of God for themselves. How can we
receive the crown of anointing oil and continue in His works for us, if we
allow ourselves to be deceived?

Ephesians 5:6-11 *Let no man deceive you with vain words:
for because of these things cometh the wrath of God upon
the children of disobedience. Be not ye therefore partakers
with them. For ye were sometimes darkness, but now are
ye light in the Lord: walk as children of light: (For the
fruit of the Spirit is in all goodness and righteousness*

*and truth;) Proving what is acceptable unto the Lord.
And have no fellowship with the unfruitful works of
darkness, but rather reprove them.*

Make Your Calling Sure

How can I make my calling and election sure with the Lord? Do you want to escape the corruption that is in this world? It goes back to being virtuous and to giving your all to the Lord Jesus. You must work on temperance, patience, godliness, kindness, and brotherly love. The Scripture gives us the formula for receiving the Lord's anointing oil. The Apostle Peter wrote in 2 Peter, Chapter 1, verses 3-10, practice these virtues: "If we do these things, *temperance, patience, godliness, kindness, and brotherly love and they are in you, furthermore abound from you, then you will not be unfruitful in the knowledge of our Lord.*"

If you lack in these areas and don't care, then you are blinded and have forgotten what the Lord purged from you while you were in sin. The Lord desires that you give all diligence and perseverance in making sure your calling from the Lord is fulfilled. If we continually live this kind of life, the Word tells us that we shall never fall. Hallelujah!

Some may think that if they cast out demons, raise the dead, heal the sick, prophesy, preach wonderfully and bring the lost to the Lord, and then they automatically get the Lord's stamp of approval. Instead, we must practice what I call it the five "P's." We think, "Well, I pray every day, therefore I am stamped with God's approval. Some days I not only pray, but I praise the Lord at least once a week at church."

What about forgiveness? "Yes, I have forgiven those, pardoned everyone who has hurt me. I pray, I praise and I pardon. Therefore, I am close to God and no one can take the Word of God out of my hand."

81

Others say, "I not only pray, praise, pardon, but I preach. I tell others about my Jesus. I preach behind the pulpit; therefore, I am special. I pray, praise, pardon and I preach!" What about pleasing God? Do you give in your tithes? This includes fivefold ministers: Do you give in tithes and offerings? This is pleasing to God. If we will do all five "P's" (pray, praise, pardon, preach and please God) every day, our lives would be so much richer with the Lord. It is much harder for someone to steal the Word of God out of your mouth and your hands if all five 'P's" are operating daily.

Too many today feel that it is acceptable to criticize the anointed ministers of Christ, those in the fivefold ministry. God calls it lawlessness. I am not saying that we should not ever, or can't question the spiritual leader who has authority over us. In any event, what we do after a disagreement is what is important. Don't let your conversation become malicious!

Matthew 15:8 *This people draweth nigh unto me with their mouth, and honoureth me with their lips; but their heart is far from me.*

2 Peter 1:10 *Wherefore the rather, brethren, give diligence to <u>make your calling and election sure:</u> for if ye do these things, ye shall never fall:*

Remember, the Lord wants to anoint us. He wants to give us His crown of anointing oil.

We must search out intent and
motives of our hearts and lives.
What does the Lord want
you to do for His glory,
for His kingdom?
How can you be an excellent
servant of God?
Find out the Father's will for
your life, do it and
He will crown you with
His anointing oil.

Acts 22:14 *And he said, The God of our fathers hath chosen thee, that thou shouldest know his will, and see that Just One, and shouldest hear the voice of his mouth.*

83

Crown of Glory

Chapter 8

Crown of Rejoicing

1 Thessalonians 2:19 *For what is our hope, or joy, or <u>crown of rejoicing</u>? Are not even ye in the presence of our Lord Jesus Christ at his coming?*

How do we receive a crown of rejoicing? In the Word, we see that Paul wasn't always welcomed with open arms. As he preached about Jesus and spread the Gospel, he was first met with great opposition and contention. The same thing happens to us today. As we bring the message of hope in Christ Jesus, the world does not want to hear the truth. Oh sure, we can talk about God in Muslim, Buddhist, Hindu, or Unity terms and **not** get stones thrown at us; however, at the very mention of the Name of Jesus, the world shuts us out. Paul's desire was to help people to realize that God not only sees what we do and what we are going to do, but that He knows our hearts and thoughts. The Lord searches the heart of His children. Our hearts deceive us, so we must constantly try them to make sure we keep holy.

Leading Someone to Christ

When we preach the Gospel and bring someone to Christ, we receive a crown of rejoicing. This crown will be given to us at the coming of our Lord. I remember the first person I led to the Lord. At the time, I was going to a women's meeting once a week at the church we were attending. There was a young woman there who had four children under the age of five and another one on the way. At first, the things that I heard at this meeting made me feel inadequate as a Christian, wife, mother, homemaker and friend. I think for the first two meetings all I did was cry. I felt like all of these other women of God really had their "act" together. I especially couldn't help thinking that I was so inadequate as a mom. As the weeks went by, I found myself focusing my attention on the young woman who had so many children. You may have heard the saying, "She had so many children she didn't know what to do." This young mom honestly didn't know what to do. When she would talk about it, she seemed calm about the whole thing. She appeared to be content, and it really didn't seem to bother her that she didn't have everything concerning motherhood figured out. I, on the other hand, was a crying mess. I always had mascara running down my face by the end of these women's meetings —I looked like a raccoon! I continued attending these meetings once a week, because I wanted to be assured that I was doing "it" right.

One morning after the meeting this young woman, whom I will call Abigail, needed a ride home. I immediately volunteered and thought, *"I will take her home and pick her brain as to find out why she seems so nonchalant about being a mother of four and another one on the way."* I only had three, and my oldest was already in school. I should be able to handle this motherhood, wife, and Christian thing. As we got closer to her home, she turned to me and asked, "Leslie, how is it that you have so much wisdom and seem to have everything together?" My mouth fell open, and if I could have fallen off the seat, I would have. Man, did I ever have her fooled! She went on, "You always have everything in place. You are dressed nicely, you have your hair in place, you even have on makeup (which came off through tears each and every time.) Your children are clean, they are dressed in clothes that match, and they seem so happy." Although still in shock, I began to tell her, "Honestly, the only way I know how to survive day by day and be the best wife, mom, Christian and friend I can be, is to pray, pray, pray. I then rejoice in the Lord in everything and anything. If you get mad and end up throwing and breaking something, you're going to be the one that has to clean it up, because you are the mom. It doesn't do any good to take the frustrations of life out on a plate or a glass of milk! Only Jesus gets me through."

As we continued our drive, all of a sudden I found myself asking her questions about her walk with the Lord. She said that she felt better about her life now that she was going to church, but she really didn't know too much about Jesus. I suddenly found myself without anything to say, I didn't know what to tell her. I remember thinking, *"How can you be going to church and not know Jesus?"* Unfortunately, I left her that evening without ministering to her and telling her how Jesus could be Lord in her life. I was scared, embarrassed, and definitely not sure what to say to her. I felt so awful inside! After she got out of the car and went into her house, I felt numb. I let her go. I had the opportunity to lead this young woman to Christ, and I messed up.

I cried out to the Lord and pleaded, "Give me another opportunity...I will do it right! I will memorize, learn the Word, do whatever it takes if you will give me another chance." When I got home, I told my husband what had happened. I asked him to direct me to the Scriptures involved in leading someone to the Lord. I wanted to make sure that I could share the Gospel effectively with someone else. There was no way I was going to miss another opportunity that my Jesus would give me. Stan gave me the following Scriptures to memorize.

Scriptures to Lead Someone to the Lord

1. Romans 3:23; we all have sinned.

   Romans 3:23 *For all have sinned, and come short of the glory of God;*

2. Ephesians 2:8-9; salvation is a gift not something to be earned.

   Ephesians 2:8-9 *For by grace are ye saved through faith; and that not of yourselves: it is the gift of God: Not of works, lest any man should boast.*

3. Romans 10: 9-10; confess with your mouth and believe in your heart.

   Romans 10:9-10 *That if thou shalt confess with thy mouth the Lord Jesus, and shalt believe in thine heart that God hath raised him from the dead, thou shalt be saved. For with the heart man believeth unto righteousness; and with the mouth confession is made unto salvation.*

4. Acts 2:38; repent and be baptized.

   Acts 2:38 *Then Peter said unto them, Repent, and be baptized every one of you in the name of Jesus Christ for the remission of sins, and ye shall receive the gift of the Holy Ghost.*

88

Stan would practice memorizing these verses with me during the week. After I had them memorized, we would role-play leading someone to the Lord. I finally felt ready! I had the Scriptures memorized, and I understood how to lead someone to the Lord. I was so grateful for my spiritual head of the household. I wasn't going to let this fish get away again.

Have you ever caught a fish? When fishing, there is a lot of waiting, and waiting, and then work. On one of our vacations, Stan and I went deep-sea fishing. I wanted so much to catch something any kind of fish. There were five of us that went deep-sea fishing. To be fair, the captain of the boat had each of us draw a card to see which fishing pole would be ours. Stan told the captain, "Well, if anyone is going to catch a fish, it will be Leslie. She has been praying diligently, and I know God answers her prayers." I was praying. I was praying hard because I wanted to catch a fish.

We had been out on this boat in the Pacific Ocean, with the sun beating down on us for about five hours. The captain said, "In 15 minutes, we're going to have to head back to shore. "I breathed a quick prayer, "Lord, I don't have much time. Help me catch a fish, please!" After that prayer, I heard the reel go wild on one of the fishing poles. I yelled, "Fish, someone has caught a fish." Then, all of a sudden I realized, IT WAS MY FISHING POLE! I went through the steps getting all the gear on I was supposed to wear for deep-sea fishing and hooked the pole in its slot. I was holding onto the pole trying to reel this big fish in. Man, it was so tough! The fish would go down deep instead of surfacing, so I had to really work at it. I couldn't believe the struggle. The thought occurred to me several times, *"I am going to go home with the fish and visit his habitation in the sea instead of him going home with me."* Even after struggling, and enduring some pain, I was about to give up, but I finally reeled that creature in! The fish came close to the boat; the captain got a hook and net and pulled it into the boat. There it was, a beautiful fish! I made it... Hallelujah!

Readers, I must admit that the fish was only a thirty pounder or so.

It was an Ahi, (yellow tuna), but it definitely felt a lot stronger and heavier than that. The muscles in my left arm were very sore for the next week. Of course I would complain about my sore muscles quite often to my husband. You see, I was the only one who caught anything. Oh, and by the way, the only woman!

This experience taught me a valuable lesson. Many times we have to go through hard work and struggles to lead someone to the Lord. We need to be prepared. We need to be ready for the struggle and not give in and give up. Sometimes its easier road is to give up and give in to our fear and not even try; but, once the fish is on board, there isn't a greater feeling, even if you are sore for a while. Jesus is our Captain. Once we have caught the fish and reel it into the boat, our Captain will bring the fish all the way on board and prepare it.

I couldn't wait for the next week to see Abigail, for I was prepared. Truthfully, I was nervous, but I knew I was as ready as I could possibly be. I called Abigail and asked if I could pick her and the children up for the women's meeting. She said that would be great, considering she wasn't going to go because she didn't have a way to get there. On the way to her house, I became very nervous and put a lot of pressure on myself. Also, the enemy kept planting thoughts in my mind. Satan would belittle and intimidate me saying, *"Who are you to preach to this woman... you won't remember the Scriptures...she'll get saved another time. Don't put so much pressure on yourself. Let someone else lead her to the Lord."* As the drive went on, more and more questions flooded my mind as to whether or not I could do this. One thing I knew for sure: it was my choice whether or not I was going to accept or reject those thoughts. I kept saying, "Lord, I know You are here and You will guide and direct every word that comes out of my mouth. Satan, get out of my thoughts, I am ready for this fish."

On the way home, after the meeting I prayed quietly, "Lord, have her ask me the right questions and help me remember all You have taught me." I drew a deep breath and began by just mentioning something the Lord had done in my life that day. Abigail replied, "Leslie I would really like to know Jesus the way you do." There it was my opening, my opportunity, and the moment I was waiting for. I was nervous, yet so excited. I asked her, "Have you ever invited Jesus into your heart and life? Have you ever prayed the sinner's prayer and believed that He would save you?"

I want you to picture this situation. When I first met Abigail, she seemed to know the Lord. Here she was, a woman who went to church every time the doors were open. She grew up attending church and appeared to have peace. What do you think her response would be? We would think that she'd say, "I don't need to pray for Jesus to come into my life; I am a good person. I go to church every Sunday. I haven't done anything wrong." Her response to me was, "I never knew I needed to pray for Jesus to come into my heart and life. I just thought I needed to be a good person and go to church." The Lord had prepared the way already, for I knew she really wasn't saved.

I led Abigail to the Lord that afternoon. She accepted Him as her Lord and Savior right there in her driveway. I had the most awesome feelings I had ever experienced. She exclaimed, "I feel good, and I feel right with God!"

Psalms 118:15 *The voice of rejoicing and salvation is in the tabernacles of the righteous: the right hand of the LORD doeth valiantly.*

I remember as I was driving away from her home saying to the Lord, "Wow, Lord, that was easy! I thought it was going to be so difficult. It was awesome!" I was so excited I couldn't wait 'til I got home to tell Stan. I was filled with joy, and I knew at the moment she received Jesus, I had to have received the crown of rejoicing. The angels in heaven were rejoicing, Jesus was rejoicing, and so was I.

1 Thessalonians 2:12-13 *That ye would walk worthy of God, who hath called you unto his kingdom and* *glory. For this cause also thank we God without ceasing, because, when ye received the word of God which ye heard of us, ye received it not as the word of men, but as it is in truth, the word of God, which effectually worketh also in you that believe.*

Luke 10:20 *Notwithstanding in this rejoice not, that the spirits are subject unto you; but rather rejoice, because your names are written in heaven.*

Luke 15:6-7 *And when he cometh home, he calleth together his friends and neighbours, saying unto them, Rejoice with me; for I have found my sheep which was lost. I say unto you, that likewise joy shall be in heaven over one sinner that repenteth, more than over ninety and nine just persons, which need no repentance.*

The Lord has given me many opportunities to lead others to Him since. I am so grateful; it's a priceless privilege I wouldn't want to be deprived of. Satan desperately tries to put stumbling blocks in our way when we are sharing the Good News, but we can be victorious and overcome the spirit of rejection, in particular, that tries to take hold. At times, a spirit of fear will try to grip you. You may have questions like, "What will happen if I mention Jesus to my family, friends and neighbors? If I bring the gospel to someone in my family, will they reject me? What about my friends? Will I lose their friendship?" Unfortunately, sometimes the answer is yes. Sometimes we will lose friends, family members, and loved ones because they don't want to hear the truth. Yet, the Lord promises that His Word will never return void. Another way of stating this is, when you speak the truth it sticks. It might take some time to see the harvest, but you stay strong and plant that seed. Obviously, you bring the message with great love. Sometimes it takes awhile to see that seed grow or get that fish in the boat!

Isaiah 55:11 *So shall my word be that goeth forth out of my mouth: <u>it shall not return unto me void, but it shall accomplish that which I please</u>, and it shall prosper in the thing whereto I sent it.*

Even in our country, sometimes preaching the gospel in the churches is frequently hindered, but when we forbid preaching to sinners we do not please God. It has become easier to compromise and go along with the sin and whoredoms of the world, than to preach the truth. We need to remember that this world is just a place we are passing through. Eternal life with Jesus is, or should be, our real goal. Loving one another to showing others the truth. Speak forth the truth of the Word of God. The Word of God is full of wisdom, holiness and truth. Let us regard His Word, the Holy Bible, in this way.

<u>**Before you even go to the next chapter my prayer is that if you don't know Jesus you will ask Him to come into your heart.**</u> Believe in Him as your Lord, Master, King, Savior, and God. He is one with the Father. Although I may never meet you here on earth, we can be assured that we'll be together in eternity. Jesus Christ will come again, and nothing will hinder His Second Coming when it is time. The problem is, we do not know when that time will be. Become a faithful minister of Christ and serve the Lord by witnessing and praying for others to know Him as their Savior, and then you will look forward with all your heart to His return.

Pray the words below out loud.

Prayer of Salvation

I, (your name) ask You Jesus, to come into my life. I admit that I am a sinner. I ask forgiveness for all my sins. I remit the sins of my forefathers and ask that they not be charged to me, my family, or generations to come. I ask you to come into my heart. Cleanse me from all unrighteousness and evil. I renounce any occult activities and deeds or participation in cults. Forgive me, Jesus, and enter my life now. I repent and turn from my evil ways. I believe that You are God. I believe that You died and arose three days later and now sit at the right hand of God, the Father. I declare that you are my Lord, my Savior, my Master, my King, my God. Thank you, Jesus, for saving me and living in me. You are the One and true living God.

In Jesus' Name, Amen!

Psalms 19:8 *The statutes of the LORD are right, rejoicing the heart: the commandment of the LORD is pure, enlightening the eyes.*

Remember to receive the crown of rejoicing. The Lord will place it on our heads at the time of His appearing. However, we can receive

94

a spiritual crown of
rejoicing right now.
The way to receive this spiritual
crown is by leading others to the
Lord Jesus Christ.

Luke 15:10 *Likewise, I say unto you, <u>there is joy in the presence of the angels of God over one sinner that repenteth.</u>*

Crown of Glory

Chapter 9

Crown of Righteousness

2 Timothy 4:8 *Henceforth there is laid up for me a <u>crown of righteousness, which the Lord, the righteous judge, shall give me at that day</u>: and not to me only, but unto all them also that love his appearing.*

We will receive the crown of righteousness on the day of the Lord's appearing. To receive that crown of righteousness, we must first understand the full meaning of being righteous. *Webster's Dictionary* refers to righteous as a means of acting in accord with divine or moral law. Someone who is righteous is free from guilt or sin and has a sense of justice or morality. A righteous person acts in a just and upright manner, and they do what is good and right. Someone with a desire to walk in righteousness is a virtuous person with good morals who is fair and just. Also according to dictionary definition, a righteous person is good, excellent, pleasant, and authentic. They are real and don't pretend to be

97

righteous. They aren't hypocrites.

The crown of righteousness will be given to us at the day of the Lord's appearing. This is one of the crowns we receive if we keep the faith. In just becoming a believer, one receives the crown of righteousness, which is actually the imputed righteousness of Jesus Christ our Lord. The Word says that it is a crown laid up for us, we don't have it yet. At the time of our deaths, or the day the Lord returns, every believer, no matter what they are going through at the time, will receive the crown of righteousness as our reward from Christ in Heaven.

We Can't Get Away with Nothin!

Satan and his demons try desperately to get us into habitual sin and rebellion...not acting in righteous ways...so that we will become guilty in the Lord's eyes. The way Satan attacks is by putting something evil in our mind. At that moment, we can either yield to the temptation and sin or reject it and tell Satan to leave us alone and rebuke him. All sin is considered unrighteousness. Have you ever (whether you are tempted in this area or not) gone into a store and thought, *"I could take that pack of gum and nobody would ever know."* I have had this happen to me. The devil is so stupid, because stealing is one of the areas I am not even tempted in. At that instant I said out loud, "I rebuke you Satan, get out of here. I will not go so low as to break one of God's commandments." The thought immediately left me, and Satan had to flee. I know people around me must have thought, "This woman is nuts!" Nevertheless, I know that there are Christians who are tempted to steal. The reason being, at one time or another they got away with stealing. At least that's what they thought.

When we open a door to Satan and sin, then the temptation in that area will increase until we decide we want to be delivered and set free. When the devil puts a thought in your mind, it is up to you at that moment whether to act on it or not.

What about gambling? I know Christians who don't have the money to buy food for their families but are tempted to buy a lottery ticket, just in case they may win. The devil has gotten us convinced that buying something as foolish as a lottery ticket might actually turn into our big break. The only break that will happen is that it will and can break a person financially. Jesus is Lord of the breakthrough - not Satan. Others may spend their life savings or paychecks at casinos. Don't fall prey to the snares of the devourer. Satan wants to devour all he can in your life and then get you really depressed.

Once I was in Las Vegas for a competition with Leslie Ann. I had a friend that loved to play the slot machines. Day after day, she would say, "Leslie, come and just play the nickel machine with me. It won't hurt. It's fun." Day after day I refused. Finally the day before we were leaving, she said one more time, "Come on, Leslie. You haven't had 'fun' the whole time." This was her idea of fun, not mine. But this time I gave in. I told her, "If I'm going to do this, I'm not wasting a nickel. I will play the one-dollar slots. I'll put only ten dollars into this machine and that's it!" I put the first dollar in, and wouldn't you know it, the machine started going crazy. Money was flying out everywhere. I thought I had broken the slot machine. I was yelling, "What happened? What did I do?" My friend was laughing and jumping around. She said, "Leslie, you just won $300.00." "What?" I gasped. I won $300.00 at that instant, but Satan won more. This is how he gets you... he entices you.

I had been thinking, *"I will spend $10.00 on this slot machine. I will not have to tell Stan that I did this gambling thing. No one will ever know."* Well, when you win $300.00 you have to tell everyone. I called Stan that night. I confessed, "Stan, I did something today you are not going to be very proud of me for doing." He replied, "How much money did you spend?" Man, it didn't take long for him to figure that out. I said, "I only spent $1.00, but, I won $300.00. Aren't you proud of me?" He had to bring me back to reality. He said, "Leslie, don't you know that was a trap of the devil? It wasn't God. All Satan has to do is allow you to win even a little, and then he can trap you into spending a whole lot more. Quit now." I did and, boy, am I glad!

I am always telling my children, "Your sins will find you out. Stay clean. You may think that you get away with sin, but the truth will be exposed sooner or later." I also tell my children that I am praying for each of them all the time. I ask the Lord to reveal any secrets, lies, or sins they may be keeping hidden. The Lord is always faithful in answering this prayer. The Lord loves them so much; He won't allow them to get by with evil. I would much rather have the Lord tell me the areas of my life that need to be cleaned up than for it to be revealed to everyone. Sometimes, though, Christians aren't very smart and think that they are getting away with sin. As the days get closer and closer to the Lord's return, the heat, so to speak, is going to be turned up on each one of us. You aren't getting away with anything! Do you want the skeletons in your filthy closet exposed for everyone to see? That will happen if repentance doesn't take place.

The Scriptures speak to us about the consequences of unrighteousness. In 1 Corinthians 6: 9-11 lists sins that make one unrighteous. The Word of God tells us if we are unrighteous, we will not inherit the Kingdom of God. I don't know about you, but if there is an area in which I'm not pleasing my Lord, then I want to change. The Word of truth tells us that we aren't to be deceived. If you are a fornicator, having sex outside of marriage or an idolater, worshipping other gods like statues, movie stars, music stars, anything that takes the place of Jesus as your first love, you will not inherit the Kingdom of God. The verses continue to say that adulterers, homosexuals, abusers, thieves, those who covet, drunkards, revilers, and extortioners will also not inherit the Kingdom of God.

1 Corinthians 6:9-11 *Know ye not that the unrighteous shall not inherit the kingdom of God? Be not deceived: neither fornicators, nor idolaters, nor adulterers, nor effeminate, nor abusers of*

*themselves with mankind, Nor thieves, nor covetous,
nor drunkards, nor revilers, nor extortioners, shall
inherit the kingdom of God. And such were some of
you: but ye are washed, but ye are sanctified, but
ye are justified in the name of the Lord Jesus, and
by the Spirit of our God.*

The life of a parent is sometimes difficult in that we don't want to embarrass our children or cause them to be uncomfortable. However, sometimes that *"Perfect Touch"* is exactly what they need. If we allow their sin to be covered up and ignored, then we teach them that this sinful response is okay.

Two examples come to mind. My daughter had a friend come over and spend the night. The next morning Leslie Ann and I had to leave early before her friend woke up. After several hours on the road we get a call from this friend. "Leslie Ann, do you know where my jeans are? I can't find them," she asked. Leslie Ann replies, "No, I saw them on the chest at the end of my bed before I left." After she hung up, I asked her what the call was all about and she repeated the conversation.

I could have just left it alone, but I didn't. I began to pray silently. The Lord revealed to me where the jeans were. I declared, "Leslie Ann, you took her jeans and hid them in your closet because you thought they were cute. You were just going to ignore her and make her think they were lost somewhere." Startled, she looked at me and started to say something, probably to defend herself, but then exclaimed, " Yes, mom that's right. I'll call her back and tell her exactly where they are. I'm so sorry." She began to cry. I asked her, "Where in the world did you get the idea that you could get away with stealing? Is this something I need to be concerned about?" She answered, "This thought entered my mind. I don't know why I did it; I just did. I know it was stupid, stupid. No, you don't need to be concerned. I allowed Satan to put a thought into my mind, and I went with it. It won't happen again."

I then told her, "You opened the door for Satan. Now he will tempt you in this area again. You will need to cast out every vain imagination that is not of God. If you ever feel weak, let me know and I will pray and help you through." I was very upset with her but also very grateful that she admitted her sin so quickly. Too many times we try to justify our actions instead of facing them and taking responsibility. We want to think that our children are so perfect and wouldn't do anything wrong. We believe that these types of situations are always someone else's fault. Don't let the devil trap you into believing this lie. Help your children realize that there are consequences for their actions and to make things right.

A young woman I know was caught in the act of molesting another child, eight years younger than she. Unfortunately, this young woman was molested herself from a very early age and now had become a perpetrator. I believe the reason she became the one committing the crime was because in all those years the sin committed against her was ignored. It was just swept under the rug, the thought being "out of sight, out of mind."

Unfortunately, as we know now, much Godly counsel and wisdom, prayer and intercession are vital to the restoration of a victim of sexual abuse. Here was a young woman, a victim who was now victimizing someone else. When confronted, she was confused and wasn't even remorseful. She was wondering what the big deal was all about. I felt so sad for her, because no one had taken the time to see to her healing and restoration. The family was Christian and felt humiliated that her name was brought before the leaders of the church. Are we just to ignore these situations? Too many times, the church would rather ignore these situations than to bring righteousness into them.

At another church a man was accused of molesting a four-year-old girl. The pastor gave this man the benefit of the doubt instead of realizing a four year old wouldn't have the inclination to lie to her mom about what had happened to her. Because the pastor chose to was protect the integrity of this man and his family, he decided not to investigate the matter further. My first response was, "What? Are you in denial pastor? He could be doing the same thing to his own children. Don't be ignorant. Do you think if we just ignore these situations they will just vanish? Let's deal with the issues and help each other. This man is sick and needs help!"

We begin to be tempted by Satan at a very early age. We are born sinners, so until we repent and accept Jesus as our Lord and Savior, we will remain sinners. We need to be cleansed of unrighteousness. Children learn very early how to manipulate parents and other adults, and it is up to us parents or leaders of the church to discipline them and correct behavioral problems.

I remember a church in which there was a woman who had very unruly children. She was a single mom, and I believe she grew immune to their behavior. These two boys would jump on the pews, run around, hide under the chairs, tip over things, run outside and aggravate other children. No one in the church would confront her or the children about their behavior. I believe the reason was because they didn't want to offend the mother. It was such a nuisance! She was so unaware of what was going on around her. Aren't we, as Christians, supposed to help each other? Aren't we admonished in the Word to help the women who are single mothers in particular?

It's My Secret!

An area of unrighteousness that is very prevalent in our churches concerns keeping secrets. I truly don't understand how, when we see a brother or sister in sin, we Christians just ignore the situation and keep quiet. Here is an example. We recently found out that a young couple of our church was smoking pot. Some of our members were aware of this, but instead of confronting the sin, they chose to keep silent, feeling as though it was none of their business. I can't understand this type of thinking. Maybe I am just a confrontational person! If we see a brother or sister in sin, we need to reveal the sin, get help if they need it, pray for them, help them repent, and get them healed and delivered!

103

1 John 5:16-20 *If any man see his brother sin a sin which is not unto death, he shall ask, and he shall give him life for them that sin not unto death. There is a sin unto death: I do not say that he shall pray for it. All unrighteousness is sin: and there is a sin not unto death. We know that whosoever is born of God sinneth not; but he that is begotten of God keepeth himself, and that wicked one toucheth him not. And we know that we are of God, and the whole world lieth in wickedness. And we know that the Son of God is come, and hath given us an understanding, that we may know him that is true, and we are in him that is true, even in his Son Jesus Christ. This is the true God, and eternal life.*

We should love our brothers and sisters in Christ so much that we let them know we want to help them. I am not talking about gossiping about them or being a "tattletale", I am speaking of getting help for our brothers and sisters in need.

Here is another situation where it is inexcusable to remain silent. I found out that a man in our congregation was verbally, emotionally, and physically abusing his wife. I went to several men of the congregation to appeal to them to step in and confront the man. Their answer was, "Leslie, it is his home and we can't trespass on his property." Excuse me men, but as a woman I just can't, and don't understand ignoring and not confronting a man whom I would consider an infidel. I'm only five feet tall and I was ready to go and *deal* with this man and the situation.

So Stan and I had them come to our office to "counsel" them. (They had previously counseled with another couple several times.) Everything seemed to be going smoothly and the man actually seemed cooperative and friendly, that is, until I pushed the wrong button. He made the comment that his wife needed to watch what she said and do whatever he told her. I turned to him, pointed my finger him and exclaimed, "I don't care what your wife says, what she does, whether she yells or talks back to you. I better not ever hear of you hitting your wife again! Is that understood?" With that remark, he was up and out of his chair and coming toward me. He and I then got into a heated debate. I told him, "I am not afraid of any demon or you. I won't stand for your unrighteousness." He began hitting my hand with his Bible in a rage. Stan got up and tried desperately to calm and ease the World War III that was going on. He said to me, "Leslie, get up and take his wife in the other room. Now!" I didn't want to. My adrenaline was pumping and I was ready to deal with this demon. Fortunately, my common sense took over and I escorted her to another room. She was so scared and panicky. She really believed her husband was about to hit me, probably because he did her. I also believe he was ready to throw a punch at me. *He was such a wimp, I could have taken him on.* Oh well.

After Stan got the man calmed down, he called the wife and me back into the office. Of course my husband was very protective and had me on the other side of this demon-possessed man, as far away as he could place me. He dealt with the man saying, "I will do everything I can to help your wife. If she needs a place to stay, we will find it. You'd better get help for your temper and never, ever hit her again."

After several more times of seeing bruises on her, we finally convinced this woman to obtain a restraining order and get her husband out of the house. What happened next is sad, but predictable. After only a few weeks she let him come home and in just a short time, things went right back to the way they were. Unrighteousness is so evil, and Satan has got such a grip on our society, even amongst Christians. We're so afraid of confronting one another in love that we just stay quiet. We are also just like the world, in the sense that we think we should just mind our own business. If we see our brother in sin, isn't it loving to help him find the truth and get set free? Also, isn't it only right that we confront someone if they are hurting another?

Like mentioned before, this woman just opened her home to this backsliding husband and will continue being abused. Why do we do these things? If we help each other and take the Godly counsel that is given to us, then it will be easier to stay free from sin. This man won't let his wife or the children come to our church anymore. He takes his family from one church to the next until either the church can't stand the unrighteousness anymore, or the heat is turned up so much he can't stay. Sometimes they have even moved to a new state to elude account-ability.

We saw one of her children recently. My son, Bentley, asked him, "Why don't you come to our church anymore?" The son's reply was, "My dad is afraid of your mom." Hallelujah! He'd better be afraid of Jesus in me.

I still get a call from the wife every so often. I told her the last time she called that the ball was in her court; she has to make the decision. She needs to decide if she's going to live the rest of her life with this man. Does she want to get a job? Does she not want to be married to him any longer, or be on her own? Either she needs to exercise these options or she needs to accept that this is the way her husband is and quit complaining about it.

Too many times we complain and complain about our lives. We have choices we can make, but many times we don't want to correct our attitudes. When difficult decisions are made, there is always heartache that has to be dealt with. This is just life. Instead of murmuring about how terrible your husband is, either accept the situation or get out, but quit bringing others into it if you really aren't going to do anything about it. I suggested to this woman that she get a job and call me in a couple of months with a decision. I haven't heard from her, so she is still with this jerk...I mean "man."

My children know that I will confront them with their sins. I will not let up until all is confessed. If I allowed them to get by with things and not push the issue until the truth is out, what kind of parent would I be? I would be allowing the enemy to have a stronghold in my child's life. Once sin is confessed, then we can be free of the unrighteousness and clean once again with our Lord.

> **James 1:16** *Confess your faults one to another, and pray one for another, that ye may be healed. The effectual fervent prayer of a righteous man availeth much.*

As a young child I remember getting by with lying to my parents. Once they let me get away with it, then I had no problems lying to them again and again. It wasn't until I was a young woman that I decided to get right with the Lord and rid myself of that sin. I didn't want telling lies to dominate my life, and when I was born again in Christ Jesus, I gave that up. Praise the Lord! Even so, it would have been much better for me as a child, to have been confronted about the lying and not gotten by with it. You see, we really don't get by with anything. Temptations will continue to follow us around. Sin is sin. It is ugly, and if we desire to have that crown of righteousness, then the race begins here on this earth. The time is <u>now</u> to start working toward the crown of righteousness.

Ugly actually means:

U	**Unrighteousness**
G	**Grips**
L	**Lives**
Y	**Young**

Matthew 18:18 *Verily I say unto you, Whatsoever ye shall bind on earth shall be bound in heaven: and whatsoever ye shall loose on earth shall be loosed in heaven.*

Throughout the Word of God, we can see that what we do here on earth will directly impact our lives in eternity. If we accept Jesus as Lord, then we will have eternal life in heaven. If we strive for righteousness in all areas of our lives, then we will receive the crown of righteousness and love the appearing of the Lord. Many heavenly rewards are determined by our actions and attitudes. When evil thoughts come into our minds, we have the authority to reject them and not give in to the temptation.

Maturing in Christ doesn't depend on our chronological age. As you walk in the Lord's holiness and as you mature in Him, you will be found more Christ-like and walk in righteousness.

Proverbs 16:31 *The hoary head is a crown of glory, if it be found in the way of righteousness.*

Striving for Righteousness!

In ancient Rome, a wreath or crown of evergreen foliage was given to those who won in an athletic competition. A crown represents becoming the winner and bestows honor on the victor. A crown in whatever form, whether a wreath or an ornate one covered in gold, is the most coveted award. The gender of the recipient doesn't matter. One thing is certain, if you accept the righteous judge, Jesus Christ, you shall be given a ***crown of righteousness*** at the day of His appearing. Maintain a steadfast love for His appearing.

Remember to strive for righteousness in your everyday walk with the Lord. Know that the Lord will help you change to become more like Him if your heart desires to do so.

2 Timothy 4:8 <u>*Henceforth there is laid up for me a crown of righteousness*</u>, *which the Lord, the righteous judge, shall give me at that day: and not to me only, but unto all them also that love his appearing.*

Crown of Glory

Chapter 10

To "B" or Not To "B" That Is the Question.

Ephesians 4:29 _Let no corrupt communication proceed out of your mouth, but that which is good to the use of edifying, that it may minister grace unto the hearers._

In 1986, when I was baptized in the Holy Spirit, I began to be mentored by several Godly women. Their prayer lives were magnificent, and I longed to be like them. They seemed to be so close to the Lord, and it always seemed like their prayers got answered. I learned to mimic the way they prayed. These ladies were mentored by others, and their mentors by someone else, and so forth. I remember a time when my spiritual mom, I will call her Diane, and I were at a Bible study. All of a sudden, she

111

stood up right in the middle of the teaching and began to come against Satan. The white chalkboard being written on kept falling off its stand, so she said in a stern voice, "Satan, I bind you in the Name of Jesus. I command you to leave, now!" Whoa, this was a bold woman, and full of authority. I wanted that kind of boldness and I surely wanted that kind of authority. I didn't understand what she was doing, but it sounded right to me. She bound Satan and loosed him.

I had and still have such zeal for God and wanted so much to be used by Him. I love to pray for people and see them free and healed from so many scars, whether they be physical, emotional, financial, or spiritual.

One time in church, a lady asked me to pray for her. This was after the Sunday morning service. We hadn't been going to the church very long, and I wasn't sure of the protocol. She declared, "I have heard you pray, and your prayers are answered. I want you to pray for me." I replied, "Okay, let's go up front to the altar, and I will pray for you there." She whispered, "Well, I thought maybe we could go somewhere else." With what was about to transpire, I am so happy that I insisted we pray at the altar. I took her up to the front near the altar and asked her, "What do I need to pray for you about?" She said, "I have this lump on my neck, and I think it is cancer. I want to be healed."

I laid my hands on the side of her neck and began to pray like I had been taught. I bound Satan in the Name of Jesus and commanded that the cancerous spirit be removed and that the tumor fall off of her. With this statement she, (actually the demon inside her) put her hands around my neck, threw me on the floor, and began choking me to death. I was terrified, but I couldn't do or say anything. I remember thinking the Name of Jesus, but that was all I could do. Several church members were still there in the sanctuary and, praise the Lord, saw what was going on. They wrestled her off of me and began praying for her. The woman was finally set free.

I want to preface the following statements by saying that God gives us grace and mercy even in our ignorance. The teaching I am about to bring you will be different for most of you. It will be a revelation to all of you. Once we know the truth about something, we are then responsible to follow through with the revelation the Lord brings us. He is such a merciful Lord and works on our behalf, even when we do not do things correctly according to the Word of God.

As I began to do a study about binding and loosing, I realized that I had not studied the Scriptures for myself nor studied about how Jesus cast evil spirits out. Once I did, I recognized that I had been praying incorrectly for many years. Nevertheless, through God's great grace He still healed many people at my request through intercession and prayer.

I want to repeat something here. Once we know a truth, we are then responsible to pray and act accordingly. **We are held accountable once we know the truth.**

> **Psalms 25:5** *Lead me in thy truth, and teach me: for thou art the God of my salvation; on thee do I wait all the day.*

> **John 8:32** *And ye shall know the truth, and the truth shall make you free.*

> **1 John 4:6** *We are of God: he that knoweth God heareth us; he that is not of God heareth not us. Hereby know we the spirit of truth, and the spirit of error.*

Bind

First, lets find out what the word *bind* actually means. According to *Webster's Dictionary*, this word means to confine, restrain, or restrict as if with bonds. To bind means to be put under obligation and constraint with legal authority. Also, the word means to wrap or fasten around. To bind is a position that restricts an opponent's freedom. It also means to hold, stick, secure, or tie together.

113

Loose

What about the word *loose*? According to *Webster's Dictionary*, this word means to cast off; to free from obligation, responsibility; to release, discharge, break up, destroy, or dissolve.

I have done an intense study of Matthew 16:19 that says, *"Whatsoever thou shalt bind on earth shall be bound in heaven and whatsoever thou shalt loose on earth shall be loosed in heaven."* So many times we only pay attention to the words bind and loose in this verses.

What is the Key?

The first part of the Scripture says, *"I will give you the keys of the kingdom of heaven."* What could be the key to understanding this Scripture? I believe the key is recognizing that in our walk with the Lord either we are free from sin or bound up in sin. We also make statements from our mouths that bind others or us to death or life. We need to realize the power we have with our tongue. For example, speaking curses like, "That just tickles me to death!" "My feet are killing me!" "You're bad!" "You're an accident waiting to happen!" You can probably think of many more statements we make that curse others or ourselves.

Proverbs 18:21 *Death and life are in the power of the tongue: and they that love it shall eat the fruit thereof.*

Only Jesus can forgive our sins, but **we can either absolve or retain sins.** If we are bound by sin on this earth we will be in heaven, and if we are loosed from sin on this earth we also will be in heaven. Being loosed is a good thing. Once we are free from sin we are joint heirs with Christ. Binding and loosing is dealt with throughout the Word of God. Jesus told parable after parable concerning either being freed or tied up. We can either be free from the bondage or loosed from it. **The Scripture in Matthew 16:19 and others with this same meaning (e.g.,** like Matthew 18:18) are not talking about binding and loosing the devil. Instead the Word is telling us we have the authority either to keep ourselves bound or free. If you bind yourself with words of death, then you are bound on earth as well as in heaven. In other words, are you bound with unforgiveness, or do you repent and become free by forgiving? You should loose unforgiveness off your life and be free. The question we must each grapple with is whether we will forbid bondage or allow it.

Everyone is a servant to some kind of master. When we are commanded to do something, we yield to the master issuing the command. We yield to either being predisposed to sin or being obedient. One is a willing slave to sin. We, who are the servants of Jesus Christ, were once slaves of sin, but now are joint heirs with the King.

> **Romans 6:19** *I speak after the manner of men because of the infirmity of your flesh: for as ye have yielded your members servants to uncleanness and to iniquity unto iniquity; even so now <u>yield your members servants to righteousness unto holiness</u>.*

In studying Matthew 18:18, I found 49 Scripture verses that have the word bind, 29 verses that have the word loose, and 474 verses with the word cast. If a dog is tied to a tree, he is bound. It is not until he is untied that he is he loosed from that tree.

In Proverbs 3:3, the Lord instructs us to not forsake mercy and truth. His Word further goes on to tell us to bind them about the neck and write them upon the table of your heart.

> **Proverbs 3:3** *Let not mercy and truth forsake thee: <u>bind them about thy neck</u>; write them upon the table of thine heart:*

This refers to an attitude of the heart. If you desire the truth of God's Word, then you love the truth. You also recognize the Lord's mercy extended to us. Not forsaking truth and mercy will require a believer to be loving and faithful. Attitude by itself is not enough. Action is required.

Think about a loving person you know. This person not only feels love, but he or she also demonstrates it in their actions. They are loyal and responsible. You can trust them. What about a faithful person? Do they demonstrate faithfulness in their life? A faithful person can be depended on to keep their word.

Another Scripture referring to binding is Isaiah 8:16.

Isaiah 8:16 *Bind up the testimony, seal the law among my disciples.*

To "bind up the testimony" and "seal the law" actually means the words of God were to be written down and preserved for future generations. As God's children we each have the responsibility of passing on the Word of God to our children, grandchildren, and so forth, generation after generation. We need to encourage those of our lineage to love the Bible, read the Bible, and obviously to learn and apply it. As we do our part, then the generations that follow us will almost surely know and follow Jesus.

Nowhere in the Scriptures did I find that Jesus ever bound a demon, Satan, or spirits of darkness. Someone might ask, "What about Isaiah 61:1?" where it says, *"He hath sent me to bind up the brokenhearted..."*

Isaiah 61:1 *The Spirit of the Lord GOD is upon me; because the LORD hath anointed me to preach good tidings unto the meek; <u>he hath sent me to bind up the brokenhearted</u>, to proclaim liberty to the captives, and the opening of the prison to them that are bound;*

The bind in this Scripture actually means to compress or medicate. The *Strong's Concordance* reference number is 2280 for this verse and defines the Hebrew term "Chabash." Chabash means to wrap firmly, compress, medicate, or to stop the hurt. This Scripture doesn't mean we are to bind Satan or his demons. We are to heal, soothe, and comfort the brokenhearted believer, according to this verse.

We believers in Jesus Christ and those who don't believe in Him must live side by side in this world. God allows unbelievers to remain for a while, just as a farmer allows weeds to remain in his field for a time. According to a farmer friend of mine, the reason a farmer allows weeds to remain for a time in his field is so when they are pulled, the surrounding wheat isn't uprooted with them. But, at the time of harvest, the weeds are uprooted.

Matthew 13:30 refers to this very thing.

> **Matthew 13:30** *<u>Let both grow together until the harvest</u>: and in the time of harvest I will say to the reapers, Gather ye together first the tares, and bind them in bundles to burn them: but gather the wheat into my barn.*

The tares are what are bound up. At the time of the end, the Lord will uproot those who are evil and throw them away to be burned. We need to continue seeking righteousness and holiness and making ourselves ready at all times to go home to be with the Lord. Make sure your faith is sincere and that you "walk the walk." Also, notice that Jesus tells the reapers to gather the tares first. The reapers are angels. At the time of the return of Jesus, He will send out His reapers, (the angels) to gather the tares (the evil) and then the wheat (the righteous). **Hmm…That does away with the pre-tribulation theory, doesn't it?**

Jesus didn't bind demons; He simply cast them out. Where did He send the demons once He cast them out? As you study the Scriptures, as I did, He did not send them anywhere. He only cast them out and commanded them to go. But, Leslie, Jesus sent them to outer darkness according to the Scripture in Matthew 22:13, right?

117

Matthew 22:13 *Then said the king to the servants, Bind him hand and foot, and take him away, and <u>cast him into outer darkness</u>, there shall be weeping and gnashing of teeth.*

I have heard many good-hearted Christians cast the demons to outer darkness, thinking that they had the authority to do so according to this Scripture. However, Matthew 22:13 is referring to the unsaved at the time of the end.

As we look at this Chapter in Matthew, in context, you will see that in Matthew 22:8 Jesus spoke to His servants and said that the wedding is ready. *The wedding feast with our Lord is not until the end.* Just as at the time of the harvest is at the end. It is not until Jesus returns are all the evil in this world and in the heaven lies without the wedding garments, sent unto outer darkness. This Scripture is future tense as to what Jesus is going to do with the unsaved.

Jesus did not have the authority nor do we have the authority to bind Satan and cast him into outer darkness, because the time of the end is not yet. We are not at the time of the harvest yet. In Matthew 25:30, the Lord cast the unprofitable servant into outer darkness. This man was thinking of only himself. This man buried his money and thought he would get away with it. This wicked and slothful servant was hoping to protect himself, but he was judged for his self-centeredness. Many times we Christians make excuses to avoid doing what God calls us to do. If Jesus is really our Master, we <u>must</u> obey Him. Our time, abilities, and money aren't ours in the first place. We are only the caretakers, not the owners. If we ignore, squander, or abuse what we are given, then we are rebellious and deserve to be punished. As we pray and desire blessings from the Lord, do you think He will give us more if we are not taking care of what He has placed in our hands right now?

Jesus commanded that demons are to loose their hold. He cast them out. We are to do the same. We don't have the authority to send them to outer darkness, to hell, to the pit, to the ground, or anywhere else. Our job is to take authority over the demons like Jesus did and command the demonic force to loose its hold and come out. Nowhere in the Word does it tell us where to send the demons. In James 4:7, we are told to resist the devil and he shall flee.

James 4:7 *Submit yourselves therefore to God. Resist the devil, and he will flee from you.*

The devil is seeking whom he can devour. He comes to steal, kill and destroy.

1 Peter 5:8 *Be sober, be vigilant; because your adversary the devil, as a roaring lion, walketh about, <u>seeking whom he may devour:</u>*

Are you available for the enemy to devour? The Scripture says he is seeking whom he can. Don't become available. We believers already have the victory. Many times, because of our rebellious nature we get all tied up in knots and fall prey to the enemy.

I have had people say to me, "Leslie, if I pray for someone else and I cast the demon out of them, I'm afraid the demon will attack me if I don't tie them up or send them somewhere. What if the demon comes back on me or someone near me?"

Casting Out Demons

1.   **First, lets remember the Word. Jesus is our example of how to cast out devils. If we pray as He did, then we need not add anything else.**

2.   **Secondly, if you are afraid of a demon attacking**

119

you, then you don't have the right to be praying for someone, anyway. We are not to fear demons; <u>they are to fear us.</u>

3. **Finally, before praying for anyone, you yourself should be free of sin and cleansed from unrighteousness. You should already have the full armor of God on. (Ephesians 6:11-18) The Blood of Jesus covering you and the Lord's ministering and guardian angels placed about you are complete protection from any harm.**

Even if we could send the demons somewhere, they wouldn't stay there because Satan is the prince of power of the air (Ephesians 2:2). A third of the fallen angels are running rampant here on earth and in the earth's atmosphere.

What about when Jesus sent the devils into the swine?

Matthew 8:31-32 *So the devils besought him, saying, If thou cast us out, suffer us to go away into the herd of swine. And he said unto them, Go. And when they were come out, they went into the herd of swine: and, behold, the whole herd of swine ran violently down a steep place into the sea, and perished in the waters.*

The devils asked Jesus to please send them to the swine. This was the only Scripture reference in which Jesus sent a demon anywhere. However, again notice; they asked and He allowed it.

In Luke 13:12, Jesus said to the woman with the spirit of infirmity, "Thou are *loosed* from thine infirmity." If you are wanting to bind anything, then I hope you see from the Scripture that you would only bind the good. Does it make sense to tie up (bind) a demon on a person? No! Does it make sense to loose a demon off a person? Yes! We want to bind people to the "good" spirits of God and loose them from the evil spirits of

120

fallen angels.

An example of this way of binding and loosing follows. If someone has a haughty (prideful) spirit, you would **loose off the haughty spirit and you would bind the contrite, humble spirit of God to them.**

Another example would be when someone has a spirit of error on them; **you would loose the spirit of error off them and bind the spirit of truth to them.** You must, however, realize that until someone wants to be free we can pray for them but they will not be delivered until they make the decision of their own free will.

There are 499 verses concerning the word spirit or spirits in the Bible. As you study the different Scriptures, you will begin to distinguish between the spirits of God and the spirits of the devil.

> **Proverbs 17:27** *He that hath knowledge spareth his words: and a man of understanding is of an excellent spirit.*

An excellent spirit is of God. The opposite would be someone who is perverse or has a foul spirit. Therefore you would **bind the excellent spirit of God to the person and loose the foul, ungodly spirit of perversion off.**

Another example is the jealous spirit. Jealousy is an evil spirit that especially loves to take root in families. If you have had sex outside of marriage or committed adultery, a jealous spirit will enter into the marriage and home. The same is true of masturbation, since this is a form of fornication. A jealous spirit has many manifestations. If someone in the home has committed a sexual crime and not repented of the evil, ungodly soul tie that was formed; a lot of anger, rage, hatred, revenge, strife, envy, selfishness, and even murder can enter the home. Watch the news reports of situations in which adultery has been committed and the terrible things the partners do to each other as a result. Remember John Wayne Bobbit? O.J. Simpson?

Food for thought; do you have children in the home with nightmares? A place to check your own life would be; has there been any sexual perversion sins opened up in the spiritual realm of your home? Is there fornication, masturbation or adultery? Once the sin is washed in the Blood of Jesus, watch the nightmares dissolve.

How do we get rid of the spirit of jealousy? It takes repenting and walking it out with the grace of God. Once you have repented, the person praying over you would **bind the spirit of the love of God and loose the spirit of jealousy.**

> **Mark 9:25** *When Jesus saw that the people came running together, he rebuked the foul spirit, saying unto him, Thou <u>dumb and deaf spirit</u>, I charge thee, <u>come out of him</u>, and enter no more into him.*

> **Romans 8:15** *For ye have <u>not received the spirit of bondage again to fear</u>; but ye have received the Spirit of adoption, whereby we cry, Abba, Father.*

This verse is clear about what to bind and what to loose. If you are in bondage to fear, then you would loose the spirit of fear off and **bind the spirit of adoption.**

The list of evil spirits below will enable you to study the subject further. It is incomplete, but is a starting point.

Evil Spirits

1. The spirit of *antichrist* (1 John 4:3)

2. The spirit of *bondage* (Romans 8:15)

3. The spirit of *fear* (Romans 8:15 & 2 Timothy 1:7)

4. *Anguish* of spirit (Exodus 6:9)

5. *Unclean* spirit (Mark 5:8)

6. The spirit of *divination* (Acts 16:16-18)

7. A *familiar* spirit (2 Kings 21:6)

8. The *dumb and deaf* spirit (Mark 9:25)

9. A *foul* spirit (Mark 9:25)

10. A spirit of *heaviness* (Isaiah 61:3)

11. A *haughty* spirit (Proverbs 16:18)

12. A *prideful* spirit (Proverbs 29:23)

13. The spirit of *infirmity* (Luke 13:11)

14. A spirit of *jealousy* (Numbers 5:14,30)

15. The spirit of *error* (1 John 4:6)

16. A *lying* spirit (2 Chronicles 18:22)

17. A *perverse* spirit (Isaiah 19:14)

18. The spirit of *whoredoms* (Hosea 5:4)

Spirits of God

1. The Spirit of the *Lord* (Judges 3:10)

2. The Spirit of *Wisdom* (Exodus 28:3)

3. An *Excellent* Spirit (Proverbs 17:27)

4. The Spirit of *Truth* (John 14:17)

5. The holy Spirit of *Promise* (Epesians 1:13)

6. The *Fruit* of the Spirit (Galatians 5:22-26)

7. The Spirit of *Power* (2 Timothy 1:7)

8. The Spirit of *Love* (2 Timothy 1:7)

9. The Spirit of *Sound Mind* (2 Timothy 1:7)

10. A *Contrite and Humble* Spirit (Isaiah 57:15)

11. The Spirit of *Holiness* (Romans 1:4)

12. A Spirit of *Faith* (2 Corinthians 4:13)

13. The Spirit of *Glory* (1 Peter 4:14)

14. The garment of *Praise* for the spirit of heaviness (Isaiah 61:3)

15. The Spirit of *Prophecy* (Revelation 19:10)

16. The Spirit of *Adoption* (Romans 8:15)

(For a further understanding of binding and loosing, the evil spirits and spirits of God, see my book entitled "Help Me! I'm All Tied Up! Binding and Loosing, Scriptural Truth.")

Remember, Jesus is our example. He commissioned us to heal the sick, cleanse the lepers, raise the dead, and cast out devils. The only way we can truly accomplish this task is to be cleansed ourselves. Perfect love casteth out all fear.

Don't allow fear to keep you from fulfilling the Lord's plan for your life. We don't need to fear demons; they need to fear us. We are Disciples of Christ. We don't need to fear.

The only fear we should have is a reverential fear of the Lord.

Matthew 10:1 *And when he had called unto him his twelve disciples, he gave them power against unclean spirits, to cast them out, and to heal all manner of sickness and all manner of disease.*

Chapter 11

I Am a Strong Man

Mark 3:27 *No man can enter into a strong man's house, and spoil his goods, except he will first bind the strong man; and then he will spoil his house.*

What is the strong man? First of all, good and well-meaning people put the two words together, instead of separating strong and man as it is in Scripture. There is a misconception that the "strongman" is actually a demonic force that has its hold over a person. I have read, as well as been taught, from some well meaning authors and speakers that the strong man is a demon. Even those who teach bind the good, and loose the evil still try to justify their mistaken teachings on this verse. If we look at **Mark 3:27**, that interpretation would be contrary to the true meaning of what binding and loosing are all about. Jesus is our example, and He never bound anything. Obviously there is more to this verse than first meets the eye.

As we read the Scripture in Mark, sentence by sentence, the first part says that no man can enter into a strong man's house. Who is the no man and who is the strong man? **Mark 3:25** says that if a house be divided against itself, then that house cannot stand. In verse 26, it says that if Satan rises up against himself, and is divided, he couldn't stand. In other words, Satan won't cast out Satan will he?

Using *Strong's Concordance* we find that the words "no man," means that nothing, (no one will be able to have the power, even the thoughts that come into the mind) will be able to enter the strong man's house. A strong man, according to the concordance, is someone strong in body, mind, and has the strength of soul to sustain the attacks of Satan. What? You mean the strong man is not demonic in nature? Not according to the Word of God. How could Satan attack Satan?

What is the house? The house is an inhabited place, a dwelling, property, wealth, or goods. So, let's put this all together. According to the Scripture, no man, which means nothing, can enter into a strong man's house. *If Satan can't enter the strong man's house, then the strong man must be you and me.* If we are believers who are strong in body and mind and have the strength to overcome Satan, then the strong man represents us.

The Scripture says, "No man can enter into a strong man's house and spoil his goods, except he will first bind the strong man and then he will spoil his house." What are our goods? Our goods refer to what we inhabit, the temple of the Holy Spirit. It is where we dwell; therefore it is our property, wealth, etc. The only way that Satan can take from us is if he comes in and puts us in bondage and binds or ties us up. If he binds us up, then he can spoil our houses.

Let's examine this verse in context.

Mark 3:25-27 *And if a house be divided against itself, that house cannot stand. And if Satan rise up against himself, and be divided, he cannot stand,* *but hath an end. No man* [Nothing, no one, will be able to or have the power, even the thoughts that come into the mind.] *can enter into a strong man's* [Someone strong in body, mind, and has the strength to sustain the attacks of Satan.] *house* [inhabited place, dwelling, property, wealth, goods], *and spoil his goods, except he will first bind* [Tie up, fasten, Satan taking possession, bind up.] *the strong man;* [One who has strength of soul to sustain the attacks of Satan.] *and then he* [Satan] *will spoil his house.* (Mark 3:25-27, emphasis added, amplication mine).

Reacting to Fear

How can Satan enter our dwelling? I believe the main doorway is fear. If we allow fear to enter our mind and we act on it, then Satan has a stronghold in our life. The only way that Satan can put us in bondage and spoil our house is if we give him the opening through sin in our lives. If we don't repent and continue in obedience, we invite the devil in.

In the Garden of Eden when Adam and Eve sinned, fear is the first thing that took root in them. Many times scholars have stated that shame and guilt was upon them. Of course this is true, but when they heard the voice of the Lord in the garden, their very first reaction, the result of the sin they committed, was fear.

Genesis 3:10 *And he said, I heard thy voice in the garden, and I was afraid, because I was naked; and I hid myself.*

Think about Adam and Eve for a moment. Would Adam have reacted in fear before Eve ate of the tree? The Scripture tells us that God gave Adam a command: "Thou shalt not eat of it." The Lord never said Adam couldn't touch the tree of knowledge. I believe that Adam loved Eve so much and desired to protect her so diligently that he wanted to make sure she didn't get near that tree! Did Adam open a door to fear because of his concern for Eve so that subtle beast of the field was able to tempt him? What exactly did God tell Adam?

Genesis 2:17 *__But of the tree of the knowledge of good and evil, thou shalt not eat of it: for in the day that thou eatest thereof thou shalt surely die.__*

The Fall of Man

Genesis 3:1-3 *Now the serpent was more subtil than any beast of the field which the LORD God had made. And he said unto the woman, Yea, hath God said, Ye shall not eat of every tree of the garden? And the __woman said unto the serpent__, We may eat of the fruit of the trees of the garden: But of the fruit of the tree which is in the midst of the garden, __God hath said, Ye shall not eat of it, neither shall ye touch it, lest ye die.__*

Where did Eve come up with "neither shall ye touch it, lest ye die?" What did Adam tell Eve? Could it be that fear entered the scene even in the perfection of the Garden of Eden? Our greatest attack from Satan has, and always will be, fear. If we succumb to the grip of Satan with any kind of fear, then he has us in bondage.

In Luke 11, we are told more about the strong man. If a strong man is armed and keeps his palace, then his goods are in peace. If the teaching is that the strong man is a demon, then how is he armed? Also, the demon cannot own the temple of the Holy Spirit, the temple being our body. Not only that, but a demon couldn't be in peace. How do we as Christians, stay armed? The first is daily prayer and communion with the Lord. We must also put on the full armor of God every single day. We especially need to handle our sword of the Spirit (the Word of God) skillfully, as well as keep our shield of faith in place at all times. Keep the joy of the Lord, which is our strength, and keep our eyes fixed on Jesus so we can keep our peace.

Luke 11:22 further elaborates on this subject. When one stronger than he (the strong man) shall come upon him and overcome him, then the armor is taken from the man and Satan divides his spoils. Who is one stronger than he? This is an evil spirit that enters the scene when we succumb to temptation and is able to overcome us. Even so, remember, we are overcomers by the Blood of the Lamb, and the Word of our testimony.

When an unclean spirit is gone out of man, the Scriptures tells us this evil spirit is seeking rest and can't find it. The evil spirit decides to enter the house or the person from which he was just cast out. When the evil spirit returns to this house, he finds it swept and garnished and (put in order). He then takes seven other spirits more wicked than himself to dwell there also. How can an evil spirit reenter someone if it finds that the person has been cleansed? The reason is in the Word. If the empty area from which this demon was evicted isn't replaced with the Word of God and the person obeying the Word, then the door is wide open. If a person wants to stay bound up, then they will. They will reopen the door to the evil spirits, and they will be worse off then they were before. A person must desire, state, and obey if they truly want to be set free. They must fill the void with the Word of God daily.

Have you ever met a Christian who lives in despair continuously? They live in self-pity, depression, and with a "woe is me" attitude? It seems that no matter what you do, say, or even pray, they will not be set free. An example of this is someone who might have an illness. They use this as a crutch to get sympathy and attention. Oh, they come up front every Sunday for prayer. They say they want to be healed. They may even be

131

slain in the spirit, but they get up and a short time later they are back where they were, complaining and murmuring. Unfortunately, these people have become comfortable with the demon that possesses, or at the very least oppresses them. They really don't want to be free of the devil. They would rather stay in the state that they're in, rather than be free. Only when someone truly desires to be set free, and stay free, will their deliverance last; otherwise, they'll remain in bondage.

> **Luke 11:28** *But he said, Yea rather, <u>blessed are they that hear the word of God, and keep it.</u>*

In **Luke 11:24-26,** Jesus illustrated an unfortunate human tendency that many of us struggle with.

> **Luke 11:24-26** *When the unclean spirit is gone out of a man, he walketh through dry places, seeking rest; and finding none, he saith, I will return unto my house whence I came out. And when he cometh, he findeth it swept and garnished. Then goeth he, and taketh to him seven other spirits more wicked than himself; and they enter in, and dwell there: and the last state of that man is worse than the first.*

To summarize, we often have the desire to reform and remove sin from our lives, but it doesn't last long. If we want the evil rooted from our lives, then we must be filled with the power of the Holy Spirit to accomplish God's new purpose for us. Stay in the Word of God, and fill the empty places!

I Am a Strong Man!

Do I Have a Phobia?

There are so many fears or phobias that people can have. A phobia according to *Webster's Dictionary* is an exaggerated, inexplicable, and illogical fear of a particular object or class of objects. Fear is a feeling of anxiety and agitation caused by the presence or nearness of danger, evil, pain, etc. Fear is timidity, dread, terror, fright, apprehension, or uneasiness. To fear is to expect with misgiving, suspect, to be doubtful.

Sometimes these phobias enter us as young children. Some are passed down through the generations, and some we pick up as adults. Some fears come upon us because of violations committed against our wills and us. Whatever the reason resulting in these fears or phobias, they are very real to people. When we get near the thing that has caused us fear, we will react fearfully.

I have a fear of lizards. I know this seems stupid, but as a child growing up in West Texas I was surrounded by a lot of lizards. It seemed like everywhere I would walk or play, there they were. These ugly little creatures haunt me. I remember one time when I was a teenager, as I backed my car out of the garage, I ran over the tail of a lizard. For days that lizard stalked me. He was always there when I would leave or return in my car. Have you ever noticed that if you don't like something, you are the first to notice it. I always see lizards before anyone else. Why, Lord? Why?

Just about anything or activity in our world can have a phobia attached to it. For example, we have all heard about the fear of heights, darkness, and spiders. What about a fear of failure or the bogeyman? Do you know that some people have *caligynephobia*? This is the fear of beautiful women. Have you heard of *arachibutyrophobia*? This is the best fear. It is the fear of peanut butter sticking to the roof of your mouth. Yes, and amen to that one! If you need an excuse to get out of the church you attend, how about this phobia? When you are really being

133

bored with the sermon and need an excuse to leave, you can say you have *homilophobia* (the fear of sermons). Don't tell your preacher I taught you that one! The list of identified phobias runs on page after page. There are so many that it's hard to count them all.

How do we get rid of fear? The Word gives us the key. When a thought enters our mind, we have at that moment the choice whether cast out every vain imagination or react to it. People with phobias believe there is a real threat to their well-being. Yes the fear exaggerated in our minds and seems so terrifying, but we, as the children of God can be rid of these fears. Don't let Satan steal your joy, peace, and wonderful walk with God by keeping you in bondage to fear.

2 Timothy 1:7 *For God Hath not given us a spirit of fear* [again to bondage]*; but power, and of love, and of a sound mind.*

If we allow phobias to torment us, how can we have sound minds? We can't. The way to freedom is through prayer, sometimes fasting, and having someone pray with us and cast the demon out. But Leslie, a Christian can't have a demon. Oh, really? We are not a sinless bunch of people. We need to strive daily to be cleansed from all unrighteousness. We allow the enemy to come in or not. I have seen demons cast out of people, yes believers in the Lord Jesus Christ, many times. Why do you think the church is full of fornicators, adulterers, sodomites, liars, and drug abusers? The reason is because they allowed the enemy to come into their house.

Matthew 12:25-29 *And Jesus knew their thoughts, and said unto them, Every kingdom divided against itself is brought to desolation; and every city or house divided against itself shall not stand: And if Satan cast out Satan, he is divided against himself; how shall then his kingdom stand? And if I by*

Beelzebub cast out devils, by whom do your children cast them out? therefore they shall be your judges. But if I cast out devils by the Spirit of God, then the kingdom of God is come unto you. Or else how can one enter into a strong man's house, and spoil his goods, except he first bind the strong man? and then he will spoil his house.

According to the Scriptures, Satan can't cast himself out. He, Satan cannot be divided against himself. Obviously this doesn't make sense when the case is made that the strong man is Satan. Satan is **not** the strong man. Satan and his workers of darkness want to bind you up. The only way he can do this is if you allow him to. The strong man is you and I. Strong man indicates man - not Satan.

This means no one, not anybody, can enter into another man's body, our temple, *except he first bind the strong man.* In this verse "he" is referring to Satan. The only way he can spoil someone's house is first to bind him up (tie him up). Satan wants to take you into captivity. He wants to put you in bondage. When evil thoughts lurk around in your mind, you either have the authority to rebuke and command them to go, or you can succumb to the temptation and go through with the sin.

As stated in Chapter 10, most sins and spirits in the Bible are either bound or loosed. For example, we can stay in darkness and bound up by unforgiveness and bitterness, or we can be free and loosed from these bondages It is up to us.

Matthew 12:33-37 *Either make the tree good, and his fruit good; or else make the tree corrupt, and his fruit corrupt: for the tree is known by his fruit. O generation of vipers, how can ye, being evil, speak good things? for out of the abundance of the heart the mouth speaketh. A good man out of the good treasure of the heart bringeth forth good things: and*

135

an evil man out of the evil treasure bringeth forth evil things. But I say unto you, That every idle word that men shall speak, they shall give account thereof in the day of judgment. For by thy words thou shalt be justified, and by thy word thou shalt be condemned.

In Luke where it says, *"But when a stronger than he shall come upon him, and overcome him..."* the question remains: Who could be stronger than we? The one that is stronger is the temptation that is overcoming you. This is why when you open the door to unrighteousness, the enemy comes into destroy you. Satan wants to put you into captivity. If in the moment, you don't stay clean and overcome the temptation, the Scripture states you will be in a worse state than you were before. The Scripture goes on to say that blessed are they that hear the Word of God and keep it. Once we are free, we are to perservere and strive to be clean. The only way that Satan can have his demons enter in someone again, is if he finds that the person is empty. This is why it is so important to stay in the Word of God, **especially** after deliverance has taken place. You must fill the empty void with the Holy Bible, King James Version.

Don't allow fear to overtake you. No matter how silly or serious the fear is, you can overcome. Franklin D. Roosevelt said, "The only thing we have to fear is fear itself." Another quote from Mohandas K. Gandhi is, "There would be no one to frighten you if you refused to be afraid." One of my favorite quotes is, "Fear is that little darkroom where negatives are developed." (Anonymous)

If you will think about some of your fears or phobias, did they start out small in your mind and have become bigger than life? I have a friend who for a long time has had a fear of doctors. The reason being, when he was a young boy his mom and a nurse held him down against his will to give him a shot. Negative thoughts entered this young boy's mind and continued to grow and develop into fear as an adult. Through prayer, we finally recognized where the fear originated. Only then was he able to release the fear. Sometimes because the fear is so deep-rooted, we do not realize where it comes from. It could be because of other children teasing you, a brother or sister, or even mom or dad. Wherever it began is where it needs to be confronted with all the authority of Jesus' Name! Seek the Lord, and He will set you free. Get the facts first, THEN panic! Just kidding. We never need to panic; we need to be free.

Remember, Jesus _is_ perfect love who casts out _all_ fear!

1 John 4:18 _There is no fear in love; but perfect love casteth out fear: because fear hath torment. He that feareth is not made perfect in love._

The only fear we should have is a reverential fear of the Lord. Proverbs 1:7 states, *"The fear of the Lord is the beginning of knowledge."* In Psalm 111:10, we are told that the fear of the Lord is the beginning of wisdom. The fear of the Lord is good and to be desired and is completely different from men's fears.

Proverbs 1:7 _The fear of the LORD is the beginning of knowledge: but fools despise wisdom and instruction._

Psalms 111:10 _The fear of the LORD is the beginning of wisdom: a good understanding have all they that do his commandments: his praise endureth for ever._

137

Remember, even though I walk through the valley of the shadow of death, I will fear no evil: for thou art with me (Psalm 23). Can a shadow hurt you? No! It isn't real. A shadow is just lurking around and is powerless. Fear no evil, for the Lord thy God is with you.

Psalms 23:4 *Yea, though I walk through the valley of the shadow of death, I will fear no evil: for thou art with me; thy rod and thy staff they comfort me.*

Chapter 12

Recognizing Differences

Revelation 3:20-22 *Behold, I stand at the door, and knock: if any man hear my voice, and open the door, I will come in to him, and will sup with him, and he with me. To him that overcometh will I grant to sit with me in my throne, even as I also overcame, and am set down with my Father in his throne. He that hath an ear, let him hear what the Spirit saith unto the churches.*

Christians open some doors in their lives, leaving them vulnerable to attacks of Satan. Some of the doors we open are due sexual sins, sanitary sins, and dietary sins. As described in Chapter 4, many of these sins (open doors to the devil) are abominations to God. Some of these abominations are harmful to our own bodies. When we realize that, then hopefully we would recognize our sin and repent...turning away from

139

these abominations.

I might as well discuss one area first and get it out of the way, before someone reading this book has an issue with it.

Deuteronomy 22:5 *The woman shall not wear that which pertaineth unto a man, neither shall a man put on a woman's garment: for all that do so are abomination unto the LORD thy God.*

There should be a distinction between man and woman. God created us to be different. As women, we are to recognize that the men are the heads over us and we shouldn't try to be like a man. Deuteronomy 22:5 isn't referring to the woman wearing slacks; the Scripture is speaking about the sin of a woman trying to become a man. Ladies, we should be honored to be the weaker vessel. This is a glorious privilege the Lord has given us. Many theologians over the years have tried to convince men and women that if a woman is wearing slacks, then this is an abomination unto the Lord. I guarantee that, Stan, my husband, wouldn't want to wear any of my pantsuits, nor would I want to wear his! This Scripture refers to much more than outward appearance and is much deeper than the surface issue of prohibiting women from wearing slacks.

Feminism or Femininity?

Women's liberation has actually brought an **un-liberated** spirit to women. I was raised in Texas where my brothers were taught to pull chairs back for ladies and help seat them. My brothers and dad would stand when a woman got up from the table or when she returned. They were taught to open house and car doors for women, no matter what their age. Nowadays, thanks to feminism, men stay away from being helpful in these ways to not offend the feminists. It has caused us ladies who still want to be treated graciously to get a bad rap. Ladies, men actually want to treat us as special. We have allowed some "good" (actually bad) ideas to take hold. We want to have our cake and eat it too. Equal pay, equal jobs, equal benefits, equal in headship...equal, equal, equal. We want equality when it serves us, not when we have to do some of the very tough work that men do.

It is well known that women can do many things at one time; due to the way our brains operate. We can wash clothes, watch TV, and talk on the phone, all at the same time. We are able to be good business partners, good organizers, good wives, good teachers, good shoppers, and good managers, etc. (see Proverbs 31). However, when we have to do things that fall outside of our realm of God-given responsibility, we eventually get burned out or overwhelmed. The reason is because the Lord made men and women to be different, and that's okay.

In 1984, I had just arrived to begin classes at the University of Kansas. This campus was much bigger than the one I had previously attended in Odessa, Texas. I had my arms full of books, carrying a purse, etc. I had finally made it to the building where my classroom was located, but right outside the door entrance, I dropped my books all over the ground. It was freezing cold that day, with snowflakes falling and ice everywhere. Here I was, little ole me, a warm-blooded Texan: freezing, overwhelmed, scared, and upset, especially since I had just dropped everything. I bent down to start picking up my books when I dropped something else. I got everything picked up again, but as people would push past me, they would knock things out of my grip once again. I was very close to tears, but I was determined to be strong and hold them. I looked around and saw all these young men just passing by and even knocking me down in their rush to get to class. They seemed to care less about helping me at all!

Finally, I asked one of the guys about to go in the door, "Will you please help me?" He looked at me strangely and then bent down and helped me gather my belongings so I said to him, "I am from Texas, and

141

there the men help us ladies...why don't they here?" His response was, "Ma'am, all one of us guys has to do on campus or in this town is try and help some girl, and we'll get chewed out, sometimes cussed out, or, even hit if we even try to be a gentleman and help them out." This really floored me; here, these women wanted to be the stronger vessels. They didn't want any courtesies extended to them. I felt like I came from Mars, not Texas! I sure wanted help. I can tell you, I welcome a man being kind and generous to me.

This all happened the first day on this campus. After my classes, I walked what seemed like miles to get to my car. I was so tired and just wanted to go to my new home. As I made my way through the parking lot and got closer to my car, I noticed that someone had broken the window on the passenger side of my car and stolen several things. I was shocked, devastated, and just wanted to go back to Texas to friendly southern hospitality. All I could do was stand there and cry. It was so cold that as tears were running down my face, they froze. Stan wasn't in Kansas yet; he was still in West Texas. My son Shawn was in daycare and I had to be there in 15 minutes to pick him up. The worst part of all was I knew no one, not a single soul in Lawrence, Kansas. All I could do was cry out to Father God, "Help me! Save me in this day of trouble Lord."

About that time, a knight in shining armor riding a white horse rode up (well okay, it sure seemed like it at the time). I would say that about him, but of course I can't because my knight would be my husband! He asked, "Miss, are you okay?" I began to tell him what had happened, and he went and got the campus police. When they arrived, these men were so kind. The campus policeman took me to a warm room and offered me the use of a telephone. The young man who was initially on the scene even called the window repair company for me. While I was speaking with the receptionist of the window repair office, we had quite a conversation! I found out that she lived really close to the daycare facility where Shawn was, and she even knew the woman actually taking care of my son. She called the daycare for me, let them know what had happened to my car and me, and they were very gracious about the whole thing. Hallelujah, there were still some nice men and women in Kansas! Apparently, at least some of the men hadn't gotten chewed out enough by the feminists!

Yuk! You women who want to be like men and think you should be treated just like them need to read your Bibles and speak with God, your Creator. Women are not to be stepped on and treated as slaves, but we are not to be in authority over men, either. This is why I pray we will never have a woman as President of the United States. We are too emotional. Sometimes we have a tough time making decisions. We tend to start a lot of different projects, get scattered and not finish any of them. When we act angry, we stay angry. If someone hurts our feelings, then that's it; we're through with them. Can you imagine all of the wars that would be started with a woman in the Oval Office? Not to mention what would happen during PMS or menopause.

Feminism actually stands for:

Female

Egos

Meddling

In

Nauseating

Inclinations

Such as

Masturbation or Manipulation

143

Godly Characteristics for Male and Female

Now that I have probably made everyone mad, remember that in Christ we are united, and have equal access joint heirs to the throne room of God. Now that's equality! The Lord will neither regard us as male or female, Jew or Greek, but only whether or not we are saved. He did, however, make each one of us unique and special. There are certain qualities and characteristics God gave men and women, which if lived out results in satisfaction and fulfillment. We need to know that whatever gender we are, it is good...God doesn't make mistakes. Femininity is wonderful, as is masculinity. Our Lord created men and women and pronounced it good.

> **Genesis 1:27-31** *So God created man in his own image, in the image of God created he him; male and female created he them. And God blessed them, and God said unto them, Be fruitful, and multiply, and replenish the earth, and subdue it: and have dominion over the fish of the sea, and over the fowl of the air, and over every living thing that moveth upon the earth. And God said, Behold, I have given you every herb bearing seed, which is upon the face of all the earth, and every tree, in the which is the fruit of a tree yielding seed; to you it shall be for meat. And to every beast of the earth, and to every fowl of the air, and to every thing that creepeth upon the earth, wherein there is life, I have given every green herb for meat: and it was so. And God saw every thing that he had made, and, behold, it was*

very good. And the evening and the morning were the sixth day.

Galatians 3:27-29 *For as many of you as have been baptized into Christ have put on Christ. There is neither Jew nor Greek, there is neither bond nor free, there is neither male nor female: for ye are all one in Christ Jesus. And if ye be Christ's, then are ye Abraham's seed, and heirs according to the promise.*

The Scripture sited above isn't doing away with the order of things in creation. It refers to your position in Christ. If you are a son of God, He is your Lord, Savior, and Master, in creation. It doesn't matter to Him whether you are male or female or what your heritage is, He sees you as His own.

Galatians 4:5-7 *To redeem them that were under the law, that we might receive the adoption of sons. And because ye are sons, God hath sent forth the Spirit of his Son into your hearts, crying, Abba, Father. Wherefore thou art no more a servant, but a son; and if a son, then an heir of God through Christ.*

As we understand who we are in Christ Jesus, then we can truly fulfill the requirements of being a believer to the greatest extent possible. What is the role of the Christian man, according to the Word of God? Man was made in God's own image. He is to be the keeper of the garden and find work to do. He is to keep the Lord's statutes and judgments. Praise and worship shall be continually coming from his mouth. A Godly man departs from evil. He is a man of understanding and faithful man who shall abound with blessings. A Godly man seeks wisdom and knowledge and fears the Lord. He is a believer in Jesus Christ as Lord, the salt of the earth, and light of the world. A Godly Christian man forgives others. He is a man of one wife and trusts her. He is known in the gates (marketplace), and calls his wife blessed and praises her (Proverbs 31). He is the head of his wife. When he finds a wife, he finds a good thing. The righteous man pleases his wife and loves her as himself. The Christian man honors his wife. He loves his wife as Christ loves the church. A man should be vigilant, sober, of good behavior, and hospitable. He should be a teacher. He shouldn't drink, be abusive, get into brawls, or be covetous. He must rule his own house well. He lives in peace with his wife. AMEN!

Men and women were both in God's own image. Husbands and wives are to be fruitful and multiply. Once a husband and wife marry, they are to leave their father and mother and the man is to cleave unto his wife. (So when you get mad at your husband ladies, don't threaten him with running home to mama!). Husbands are to render unto their wives due benevolence, and wives are to do the same. Neither husband nor wife is to have power over his or her own body. In other words, if the husband desires to be intimate and make love, the wife should submit. The same is for the husband. If the wife desires sexual fulfillment, the man is to not deny her either.

Wives will desire their husbands. The Christian woman should strive to be virtuous. She is the caregiver of her children and should always please her husband. The woman is to reverence her husband. She is to be the keeper of the home. She rises early to get things ready in her home. She is to stay busy and not be idle. Older women will be teachers of the younger women. A prudent woman is pleasing to the Lord. The woman is to reverence her husband.

As we have a clean heart before the Lord regarding our marriages, we will be blessed. The Scripture speaks of not going to bed at night if there is any anger between husband and wife. When there is a conflict in the home, the man usually wants to walk away and not deal with the issue. He would rather go and calm down alone. But... the woman wants the man to *pull* her feelings out of her right then and there. She wants to have the conflict resolved, but wants her husband there to help. You can see the controversy that can arise because of these differences. After a man says what is on his mind, he can then go right off to sleep and not think another thing about the argument. On the other hand, the woman will toss and turn all night and let the pain fester inside her. She will get <u>more</u> upset as the hours go by. The next morning the man will probably think that everything will be normal, but the woman will be holding a grudge. The issue has not been resolved in her mind, because she didn't get the chance to "discuss" the problem enough.

Women, we need to say what we want five times and make sure you men have heard every word at least five times in a row. We want to make sure you are listening! As we return to the scenario discussed above, the man has no idea there is still a problem. He can't even remember what the argument was about. An entire night, all night long, eight hours has passed. In retrospect, the woman can tell you every little detail of how the argument started, what he said, what she said...I'm telling you, she can remember it all. I believe this is why the Lord said to not let the sun go down on your wrath. The bitterness and anger will continue to worsen until the issue is resolved. Men, a little advice: I know that you would rather ignore the argument and hope the whole thing will go away, but if you want to have a better relationship with your wife, you will help her release the hurt by talking things out. Believe me, you will be a much happier man in the long run!

Men are fixers. They want to fix a problem. That is why, in the heat of the argument, they need to get away. They want to think things out, find the solution, and be done with the whole matter. For example, I get almost afraid of telling Stan that I have a headache. What I want is just for him to hold me and say, "It's okay honey, I'll take care of you. Do you want me to get you some aspirin? Do you want me to rub your back? Do you want to go shopping?" Anything...just give me attention! Instead, he goes to the kitchen to fix some kind of disgusting thing for me to drink to help my headache. Then come the questions. What did you eat today that maybe caused this headache? What, what, what? I just wanted a hug! You know what, though? God made men so special. They are problem solvers. Praise the Lord! I am glad that men are problem solvers and stay focused. That is a blessing for women, if they will only accept it.

1 Peter 3:7 *Likewise, ye <u>husbands</u>, dwell with them according to knowledge, <u>giving honour unto the wife, as unto the weaker vessel</u>, and as being heirs together of the grace of life; <u>that your prayers be not hindered</u>.*

Remember, to be blessed in your relationship, you must lay your own thoughts and desires on the altar.

We need to be unselfish and giving

to our mates.

1 John 3:16 *Hereby perceive we the love of God, because he laid down his life for us: and we ought to lay down our lives for the brethren.*

Chapter 13

Robe of Righteousness

Isaiah 61:10 *I will greatly rejoice in the LORD, my soul shall be joyful in my God; for he hath clothed me with the garments of salvation, <u>he hath covered me with the robe of righteousness</u>, as a bridegroom decketh himself with ornaments, and as a bride adorneth herself with her jewels.*

To put on a robe of righteousness means that if we want eternal life (salvation) we must strive to walk in righteousness right now in this lifetime. Some Christians believe the once saved, always saved theory, the premise being that if I confess Jesus as my Lord and Savior today, even if I will fully live in sin tomorrow, I will be saved. The Word of God says to repent. This means that you must turn completely away from your sinful nature. A daily cleansing must take place. Just as we can get dirt on our bodies daily, we also pick up dirt in the spiritual sense, because we are

149

all sinners. Does it make sense to say, "Jesus, save me. I believe that you died for me, arose three days later and You are my Lord. I am a sinner." and then continue to live like the devil? Obviously a sin free life isn't achieved instantly, it's a step-by-step process. The Lord doesn't expect us to be perfect once we are saved, but we make daily choices whether be continually cleansed or live in sin. We have the choice to accept Jesus Christ or deny Him. The Lord won't override our wills. He gives us choices. If we choose Him today, He is our Savior. If we deny Him tomorrow, we go to hell because we have the choice if we are going to make Him Master and Lord or not.

1 John 1:8-10 *If we say that we have no sin, we deceive ourselves, and the truth is not in us. If we confess our sins, he is faithful and just to forgive us our sins, and to cleanse us from all unrighteousness. If we say that we have not sinned, we make him a liar, and his word is not in us.*

The Word of God tells us that our names **can** be blotted out of the Lamb's Book of Life. Our names are written in the Book of Life when we are saved but Jesus Himself said if we don't overcome evil then our names could be blotted out. We have an awesome responsibility to daily cover ourselves with the robe of righteousness once we accept Jesus as our Savior.

Revelation 3:5 *He that overcometh, the same shall be clothed in white raiment; and I will not blot out his name out of the book of life but I will confess his name before my Father, and before his angels.*

To continually put on the robe of righteousness, we must have patience and faith. Our bodies are temples of God.

1 Corinthians 3:16 *Know ye not that* <u>*ye are the*</u> <u>*temple of God*</u>*, and that the Spirit of God dwelleth in you?*

Why do we have wear a robe in the natural, the first reason to wear a robe is that it covers us. It also keeps us warm. How about wearing one just for comfort and relaxation? A robe shouldn't be worn just to look at. As a woman I own several robes. A few of them are very beautiful. Some are very thin and feminine. Then, there are my favorites, the ones that are warm, worn out, faded, ugly, stained, and comfortable. When I have company and need to cover myself with a robe, I certainly don't put on one of my old favorites! I put on one of the lovely and appropriate ones, one that is clean, pretty, and covers well. This is similar to the Lord putting the robe of righteousness on us. As we strive to live a righteous life, we often feel worn out, tired, and stained from the blood battle we engage in. We also have stains of sin on our robes that are hard to remove. We can end up getting comfortable in our fleshly ways of living. Even so, the Lord wants to put on us a beautiful garment, a freshly laundered robe, and one that is clean and appropriate.

We must be overcomers. We must flee from sin. When Satan comes to you and whispers something in your ear, at that moment you have the choice whether to listen and obey that strange voice or rebuke the devil and tell him to flee. To be an overcomer means to master, prevail and conquer. To be an overcomer, you render the enemy helpless. The overcomer will win spiritual battles and be victorious.

We need to always remember that the devil's power and his success is limited. It is even limited by how much power we yield to him. Make sure you are a member of the Remnant, redeemed by the blood. Are you a saint of God and sealed by the Holy Spirit? The devil will try to come again and again to defeat you through the weakness of the flesh; however, Satan and the principalities and powers can't prevail against a disciple of Jesus Christ. We must persevere in our faith and the application of the Word of God to be victorious over the temptations and trials we face.

151

Jesus proclaimed that the gates of hell shall not prevail against us.

Matthew 16:18 *And I say also unto thee, That thou art Peter, and upon this rock I will build my church; and the <u>gates of hell shall not prevail against it</u>.*

There is fornication and all types of sexual immorality in the Church. As the body of Christ, we must overcome our fleshly desires and work towards living a clean and righteous life. You choose daily whether or not you will put on the robe of righteousness. Be completely determined that you will *never* again do the things that would cause our Lord to be ashamed.

1 Corinthians 6:13-20 *Meats for the belly, and the belly for meats: but God shall destroy both it and them. Now the <u>body is not for fornication, but for the Lord</u>; and the Lord for the body. And God hath both raised up the Lord, and will also raise up us by his own power. Know ye not that <u>your bodies are the members of Christ?</u> shall I then take the members of Christ, and make them the members of an harlot? God forbid. What? know ye not that he which is joined to an harlot is one body? for two, saith he, shall be one flesh. But he that is joined unto the Lord is one spirit. <u>Flee fornication.</u> Every sin that a man doeth is without the body; but <u>he that committeth fornication sinneth against his own body.</u> What? know ye not that <u>your body is the temple of the Holy Ghost</u> which is in you, which ye have of God, and ye are not your own? For ye are bought with a price: <u>therefore glorify God in your body, and in your spirit, which are God's.</u>*

152

Apparently, in Paul's address to the Corinthians, it seemed they thought they could do just about anything they wanted. While it is true that there is liberty and freedom with the Lord, we are still required to be instruments of righteousness and holiness before our Lord if we are Christians; we are never to be used as instruments for sin. Our goal should be to keep from dishonoring our bodies and minds by yielding to fleshly lusts. We are to glorify God in our bodies and spirits, which belong to the Lord.

> **Isaiah 61:10-11** *I will greatly rejoice in the LORD, my soul shall be joyful in my God; for he hath clothed me with the garments of salvation, <u>he hath covered me with the robe of righteousness</u>, as a bridegroom decketh himself with ornaments, and as a bride adorneth herself with her jewels. For as the earth bringeth forth her bud, and as the garden causeth the things that are sown in it to spring forth; so the Lord GOD will cause righteousness and praise to spring forth before all the nations.*

Prepare for Righteousness

As born-again believers, we must respond to the laws of God. Just as a bridal pair are prepared and adorned for marriage, the believer must be prepared for righteousness. When you put on the robe of righteousness, you make a decision; the decision to do what is morally correct, the decision to follow the laws of God, the decision to love not hate, and the decision to follow Christ by always determining to strive for holiness.

A bride prepares herself for her groom. On the day of her wedding, it is not uncommon for the bride to start getting ready hours before the ceremony. There are countless days of preparation that a woman undergoes to have the perfect wedding she has been dreaming about all of her life. On the day of the marriage ceremony, the woman will cleanse herself from the top of her head to the bottom of her feet. The bride will cover herself with sweet smelling lotion and perfume. She will make sure that every hair is in place and her makeup is perfect. Before even getting to the wedding gown, many other things must be put on first. There are nylons, undergarments, a slip, necklace, earrings, shoes, veil, and finally the wedding dress. The wedding gown is the last thing the bride puts on. The reason it is last is because the bride doesn't want the dress to be spoiled in any way.

The groom prepares himself for the bride by showering, shaving, combing his hair, putting on his tuxedo and shined shoes. He also prepares himself to look his best for his bride. This is analogous to righteousness in the believer's life. We prepare ourself for His glory. Walking in righteousness is a day-by-day walk. If we are to wear the garments of salvation for all eternity, we must be covered with the robe of the Lord's righteousness now by being conformed to His image daily. This requires renewing our minds with the Word of God every day. As we also continue in daily earnest prayer, the Lord will cause righteousness to spring forth amongst His people.

Isaiah 51:5-8 *My righteousness is near; my salvation is gone forth, and mine arms shall judge the people; the isles shall wait upon me, and on mine arm shall they trust. Lift up your eyes to the heavens, and look upon the earth beneath: for the heavens shall vanish away like smoke, and the earth shall wax old like a garment, and they that dwell therein shall die in like manner: <u>but my salvation shall be for ever, and my righteousness shall not be abolished.</u> Hearken unto me, ye that know righteousness, the people in whose heart is my law; fear ye not the* *reproach of men, neither be ye afraid of their revilings. For the moth shall eat them up like a garment, and the worm shall eat them like wool: but my righteousness shall be for ever, and my salvation from generation to generation.*

The Lord's salvation is available to us now and forevermore. Be a part of His Kingdom. The Lord's righteousness shall never be abolished. It will endure forever. If we abide in Him and He in us, then we will be comforted in the perilous days to come. Even when the earth shall be shaken and lost and when the sky seems to disappear like smoke, those of us who dwell in the Lord's righteousness and salvation shall live forever, while the unrighteous will live in darkness.

Remember in order to be clothed in righteousness, we need to seek to be conformed to the Lord's image.

2 Corinthians 5:21 *For he hath made him to be sin for us, who knew no sin; that we might be made the righteousness of God in him.*

Crown of Glory

Chapter 14

The King Greatly Desires Beauty

Psalms 45:11 *So shall <u>the king greatly desire thy beauty</u>: for he is thy Lord; and worship thou him.*

Our King the Lord Jesus Christ, greatly desires that the beauty of holiness characterize His children. How do we become beautiful in His eyes? Beauty consists of behaviors that please and satisfy our Lord. Esther was looked upon as someone who was beautiful in the eyes of a king and his kingdom. She was chosen not solely because of her outward beauty, but I believe the king was drawn to her inward beauty as well. She not only had favor with God, but with men, also.

Beauty not only pertains to the woman. Every man, woman and child needs to have a renewed spirit man develop inside them. When we

157

are born again by the Spirit of the Living God, we are created anew. We become beautiful to the Lord. At that moment our hearts don't automatically become right and good, but we do receive new hearts. We receive a new desire to be holy, to walk in righteousness, and to have a clean life. Yes, even though we may fall, He is always there to pick us up and clean the dirt off that has accumulated in our lives.

Beauty is the result of the workmanship of Jesus on us. He begins to build His character and conduct into obedient believers. Some synonyms of beauty include attractiveness, exquisiteness, grace, refinement, loveliness, blessing, excellence, and importance. Since beauty comes from the Lord it is not found in the outward appearance, but in our inner parts. However, we can see by the different words that describe beauty that others will want to be near someone who has the beauty of holiness. Have you ever found that you are drawn to someone and don't really know why? You start talking to them and discover they are a Christian. The reason for the drawing is the loveliness and beauty of the Lord radiating from them. You are actually drawn to Jesus in them, not the person.

> **Matthew 12:34-37 *O generation of vipers, how can ye, being evil, speak good things? For out of the abundance of the heart the mouth speaketh. <u>A good man out of the good treasure of the heart bringeth forth good things:</u> and an evil man out of the evil treasure bringeth forth evil things. But I say unto you, That every idle word that men shall speak, they shall give account thereof in the day of judgment. For by <u>thy words thou shalt be justified, and by thy words thou shalt be condemned.</u>***

The Lord knows the secrets of our hearts and no matter how we appear outwardly, He knows our every good and evil thought.

The King Greatly Desires Beauty

Psalms 44:21 *Shall not God search this out? for <u>he</u> <u>knoweth the secrets of the heart</u>.*

Since beauty is manifested from the inside out, one's outward appearance will reflect their inner spiritual state. Haven't you heard people say, "Her countenance looked really hard," or "Look how his/her countenance has changed!" What they are saying is that someone in bondage looks hard, cold, unresponsive, perverted and evil. When someone has the bondages of Satan lifted off them they look alive and happy, their smile is genuine, there isn't that wrinkle in the forehead that shows despair, and they're not frowning. Go and look at yourself in the mirror. Do you look hard and cold or loving and soft? Are you smiling or frowning? Do your smile lines turn downward?

When I was very young, my mom would put my brother Nicky and me down for a nap. Many times she would say, "I will give a prize to the first one who goes to sleep." We always knew that it was going to be a candy bar. Each time she said this, it was music to my ears! At night before I went to sleep, I would practice how to position my mouth so that it wouldn't look like I was smiling. I was afraid if whoever checked saw a smile on my face, they would know I was pretending. I hated taking naps, but I loved getting those candy bars! I would practice each evening at bedtime, so I could win that candy bar the next day. And by the way, I usually did. My mom would send someone in to check on us to see if we were asleep. My brother would try to pretend he was sleeping, but he never got away with it. They would catch him bluffing, then look over at me. I looked like I was asleep, but I actually wasn't. The housekeeper would place the candy bar under my pillow and leave. My brother then really would fall off to sleep, and I would sit up and eat my candy bar.

These days, women and men are consumed with their looks, especially in this country. Sometimes we become so preoccupied with our looks that we actually become very unhealthy because of inadequate diets to starve our way to being thin. We wear too much makeup in our

159

attempts to look like a movie star. We become haughty and prideful, obviously this isn't good! It is, however, important to be clean and to represent Jesus well. We need to be a good witness for Him. If a Christian is filthy, stinks with body odor, has unkempt hair, yellow teeth, bad breath, or vulgar clothes, whether too revealing or torn and dirty, people won't want to be ministered to by someone like that. We need to be well kept. Yes, beauty comes from the inside out, but the outward appearance still matters. My mom, probably like yours, said that, "Cleanliness is next to Godliness."

When one has a teenage daughter nowadays, it is difficult to shop for her. The "in-style" clothes are revealing, tight, low cut, see through, or short. I remember when I was a teenager the clothes were almost as bad. It is time to teach integrity, purity and righteousness to our young ladies. Church leaders need to teach about purity and modest appearance from the pulpit. Parents need to teach it at home. They won't get taught about these subjects at school.

Females were created to desire men. Many think that the only way they can get one to notice them is by wearing something revealing. As a young woman I remember thinking the same thing. We might get a man by dressing this way, but it surely won't be the type of attention we really want from him. Many young women have poor self-images. This can be one of the reasons they dress inappropriately.

> **Isaiah 4:1** *And in that day <u>seven women shall take hold of one man</u>, saying, We will eat our own bread, and wear our own apparel: <u>only let us be called by thy name, to take away our reproach</u>.*

Too many times I hear the statement, "God looks at the heart, not on the outward appearance." This is, ultimately a cop-out. It is true to the extent that God is not concerned with whether we are wearing our tuxedos and evening gowns, or jeans and a tee shirt. Nevertheless, I challenge those women who choose to dress like prostitutes, or men that dress like slobs, to truly check your hearts. Are you dressing that way to get attention? Are you dressing that way to be rebellious? Are you dressing that way because you have a poor self-image? Are you dressing inappropriately because your heart is not pure before Jesus? The question you need to ask yourself sincerely and honestly is, "Would Jesus approve of my appearance? Would He approve of the way I dress?"

When you are representing Jesus by living a righteous life, you will have a glow about you. People will be drawn to you. You will have a natural smile on your face; you won't have to practice your smile like I did as a child. The beauty of Jesus will just burst forth. You are the temple of the God. If you are a clean vessel then it is actually Jesus shining forth through you. The people that are drawn to you actually see Jesus in you.

As we get closer to our Lord, study His Word, and strive to live righteously, a beauty will shine forth through us. He shows us in His Word the issues of life and what the heart of a righteous, beautiful man looks like.

Proverbs 4:23-27 *Keep thy heart with all diligence; for out of it are the issues of life. Put away from thee a froward mouth, and perverse lips put far from thee. Let thine eyes look right on, and let thine eyelids look straight before thee. Ponder the path of thy feet, and let all thy ways be established. Turn not to the right hand nor to the left: remove thy foot from evil.*

Sometimes evil appears to be good and pleasant, but the end result of yielding to it won't be pleasant. If we are tempted by something of someone, we need to keep it/them at a great distance. You can't get too far away from temptations. Wickedness is dangerous, and we need to learn how to avoid it. We are to keep our heart with all diligence. In other words, guard it and keep ourselves from partaking of evil things. When

161

the Lord instructs us to put away a froward mouth and perverse lips, He doesn't just say to not have these things, but put them away. When you put something away, you don't see it anymore. It isn't within your grasp. The old adage, "out of sight, out of mind" applies here. Froward means to be habitually disposed to disobedience and opposition. Perverse means to turn away from what is right or good. Someone with a perverse spirit is actually doing something contrary to the evidence or the direction of the judge on a point of law. Jesus is the righteous Judge. Anything contrary to His laws is perverse. Also someone with a perverse spirit is obstinate, stubborn and cranky.

The Holy Spirit in us let's us know when we have done something wrong. We can either ignore the prompting or respond to it. If we continue to ignore conviction, our hearts become hardened and we won't respond the right way. The Holy Spirit eventually will stop prompting us to do what is right if we continue to ignore Him. God gives us choices. We have the choice whether to respond to the Holy Spirit's prompting us toward righteousness or ignore Him.

Turn Your Head from Evil

Our eyes should be turned away from vanity (see the book Ecclesiastes), looking straight ahead, and walking in the counsel of God's Word. The steps we are to follow are our Lord's, our Master's, our King's. Don't even step foot into the paths of evil. The Lord will forgive our past and enable us to be obedient in following His guidelines.

Proverbs 15:28 *The heart of the righteous studieth to answer: but the mouth of the wicked poureth out evil things.*

I remember seeing a man on Christian TV who wasn't pleasant to

162

look at. His face was really messed up from a grenade exploding in his face during his tour in Vietnam. He looks like something from a Frankenstein movie. Even so, the love and beauty of Jesus that pour out of this man is incredible! When I first noticed his outward appearance, my natural inclination was to turn the channel. It almost made me sick to my stomach when I looked at him; but, I felt I was really supposed to pay attention to what this man had to say, so I continued to listen to him. As I was watching, I forgot what he looked like on the outside, and I saw Jesus. He is a righteous man with a powerful message for the Lord's people.

Here was someone who had some very unfortunate things happen to him. He wasn't even expected to survive this terrible event, but the Lord had other plans for him. He has a miraculous testimony that has touched thousands; he is a man with a God-ordained mission.

Our Father God's loving kindness and mercy endures forever. The Holy Spirit leads us, God's children, in the way of righteousness. We are born sinners, and the way to be beautiful in His eyes is to repent of the evil of sin and seek out the beauty of holiness. As we grow intimate with the Lord and His holiness, we will lose the desire to continue in sin. Some Christians have a greater sense of security in the Father's love, while others struggle in this area. Be encouraged...know that Jesus is full of grace and mercy. He is loving, forgiving, and incredibly patient with His children.

We, the church of true believers, are compared to a Queen who wears a crown. The Lord has an everlasting covenant with us. We are His Bride, the Lamb's wife, to whom He has given much grace.

Psalms 45:6-9 *Thy throne, O God, is for ever and ever: the scepter of thy kingdom is a right scepter. <u>Thou lovest righteousness, and hatest wickedness:</u> therefore God, thy God, hath anointed thee with the oil of gladness above thy fellows. All thy garments smell of myrrh, and aloes, and cassia, out of the*

163

ivory palaces, whereby they have made thee glad. Kings' daughters were among thy honourable women: upon thy right hand did stand the queen in gold of Ophir.

As the Lord prepares his Queen, His Bride, (His children), He says we will wear the finest of garments, have a wonderful fragrance, will be pure, and will be like gold. We owe our redemption to the precious Blood of the Lamb.

If your life is filled with inward enmity toward God, then it will be apparent on the outside. If you are filled with bitterness, strife, jealousy, anger, there will be every evil work in your life. As we turn toward holiness with a desire to be spiritually perfect or pure and untainted by evil or sin, then enmity towards the Lord and each other fades away.

Remember, beauty is from the innermost part of our very being. Tame the tongue to speak good and not evil.

Do not forget to:
SMILE!

When you smile, you will become:

Someone
Most
Inclined to be
Lovely
Everyday

Psalms 45:11 *So shall the king greatly desire thy beauty: for he is thy Lord; and worship thou him.*

Crown of Glory

Chapter 15

Tried, But Not Destroyed

James 1:12 *Blessed is the man that endureth temptation: for <u>when he is tried, he shall receive the crown of life</u>, which the Lord hath promised to them that love him.*

Revelation 2:10 *Fear none of those things which thou shalt suffer: behold, the devil shall cast some of you into prison, that ye may be tried; and ye shall have tribulation ten days: be thou faithful unto death, and I will give thee a crown of life.*

Oh Lord, help us to endure temptation. What kind of vexations are you enticed by? Could it be lust, overeating, cursing, rebellion, controlling, anger, pouting, manipulation, pride, dictatorship, any kind of sexual

167

sin, drugs, alcohol, lying, murder or hatred? This list by far is not near complete and could go on and on. There is not one of us who likes to be subjected to temptation and troubles. Whatever our besetting sin is, whatever our thorn in the flesh, the Lord will often allow us to experience the attacks of Satan to try us and compel us into choosing between right and wrong. As we go through trials and tribulations, the Lord sometimes seems very far away, yet the Word says He will never leave us nor forsake us. How can we endure? How can we obtain the necessary strength to overcome? Some give up in defeat too soon, some go completely back to their old way of life, and some persevere and get through.

Look at it this way. Every step you take toward enduring the trouble, the closer you get toward fulfilling the high call God has on your life. If you give up you lose ground. I don't know about you, but I don't like to lose. Actually, I don't know anyone who likes to lose. I know some who would rather give up then try harder, but that is outright laziness. That is giving in to the temptation. That is being a wimp and thinking, "I can't take the pain anymore." Don't get me wrong, there have been many days when I felt like this, but something rises up inside me, and Satan then loses the match. <u>I refuse to let the devil win</u>. I refuse to give in to the trial or temptation. The enemy wants us to give up so he can devour us! He wants us to give up so that we lose our *Crown of Life*.

Endure Temptation

What does the Lord mean when He says, "Blessed is the man who endureth temptation?" How can going through trials and troubles be a blessing? The reason it is a blessing for those of us who endure the temptation is because we become more Christlike at the end of that trial. The fleshly desires are melted away. Yes, it hurts our flesh (our bodies and souls) to go through the fiery furnace, but the Lord is always right there with us. What the Lord allows to happen to each of us who overcome, is to become more motivated by the Holy Spirit than the flesh. The Holy Spirit dwells in us when we accept Jesus as Lord. He also baptizes us with His Spirit to those who will ask. This is a gift from the Lord.

Do I have the baptism of the Holy Ghost if I have received Jesus and was water baptized? The Word of God says;

> **Luke 3:16** *John answered, saying unto them all, I indeed baptize you with water; but one mightier than I cometh, the latchet of whose shoes I am not worthy to unloose: he shall baptize you with the Holy Ghost and with fire:*

> **Acts 1:8** *But ye shall receive power, after that the Holy Ghost is come upon you (THE BAPTISM OF THE HOLY SPIRIT): and ye shall be witnesses unto me both in Jerusalem, and in all Judaea, and in Samaria, and unto the uttermost part of the earth.*

Asking for the baptism of the Holy Spirit gives us the ability to prophesy, and we receive nine <u>gifts</u> of the Holy Spirit. The Scripture according to 1 Corinthians 12:8-10 defines these gifts. They are word of wisdom, word of knowledge, faith, gifts of healing, working of miracles, prophecy, discerning of spirits, divers kinds of tongues, and the interpretation of tongues. John baptized with <u>water</u> for repentance. Jesus baptizes with <u>Spirit</u> for boldness, power, and to be a witness. All you need to do to receive the baptism of the Holy Spirit according to Acts 8:17, is to have a believer, filled with His Spirit, lay hands on you and you ask for the baptism. How do I know if I received the Holy Ghost? Look at the following Scripture.

> **Acts 2:4** *And they were all filled with the Holy Ghost, and <u>began to speak with other tongues</u>, as the Spirit gave them utterance.*

169

The initial evidence and continued evidence is speaking in tongues. Remember, He gives you all nine of His gifts at the infilling of His Spirit. If He will give you the least of the gifts, you know you receive all the other gifts.

How Do I Get the Holy Ghost Baptism?

1. <u>Repent</u> of all sins and receive Jesus as Lord and Savior.

    Acts 2:38 *Then Peter said unto them, Repent, and be baptized every one of you in the name of Jesus Christ for the remission of sins, and ye shall receive the gift of the Holy Ghost.*

2. Be <u>prayed or breathed</u> on for by someone who has it.

    Acts 8:17 *Then laid they their hands on them, and they received the Holy Ghost.*

    John 20:22 *And when he had said this, he breathed on them, and saith unto them, Receive ye the Holy Ghost:*

3. <u>Ask</u> for the Baptism.

    Luke 11:13 *If ye then, being evil, know how to give good gifts unto your children: how much more shall your heavenly Father give the Holy Spirit to them that ask him?*

170

4. Get hands laid on you.

5. Want to receive it and Jesus will give it!

What would hinder me from receiving the Baptism of the Holy Spirit?

1. Unforgiveness
2. Bitterness
3. Hate
4. Ought (disagreement) with your brother in Christ.
5. Doubt and unbelief
6. Robbing God in Tithes and Offerings
7. Misunderstanding the purpose. (To go to work for God in power, boldness, and to be a witness.)

The problem is we do not always give Him the freedom to guide and direct us. We want things our own way rather than what the Lord wants. The good news is that the Lord says we overcome, we win a crown. The Christian who has been tried and endured will be blessed and crowned by the Lord Himself. The reason the Lord promises that we will receive the crown of life is because we have the love of God reigning in our hearts.

In today's society, it seems as though the devil's crowd has all the wealth, the big homes, nice cars, all the women or men that they would ever want, and the appearance of fantastic, fun-filled lives. It doesn't matter how much money or fame you have, without Christ <u>you will be miserable</u>. That is why the devil's crowd turns toward drugs, alcohol, and all the sexual sins.

As we go through trials and "spankings" from God, our character

171

begins to change. This should evoke a "Praise the Lord!" He wants us to become more Christlike. He wants us to become stronger in Him. Christianity teaches us to be joyful under all circumstances. If we endure the rough circumstances and let patience have its work in us, instead of yielding to passion or becoming lethargic, then we will see that when we have passed through the fiery trials everything that is necessary for victorious spiritual warfare has been thoroughly furnished to us.

If we pray for the removal of affliction and troubles, we will never learn the ways of the Lord. One way to endure is to remember that pleasures of the world will fade away and ultimately be destroyed, but eternal life and the crown of life endure forever.

One thing I have observed from going through my own trials and witnessing others' is that their purpose is to remove the sinful nature of man. Enduring trials also removes the desire for things of the world. As we go through trials and tribulation, our fleshly desires are burnt off, which hurts! It feels miserable! Nevertheless, once we get through the tough times, we can look back and say, "Thank you, Lord, for helping me through. Thank you, Lord, for changing me and making me different." We should never let the circumstances of our lives, whatever they are, keep us from rejoicing and praising the Lord. Every one of us who truly love God will have trials in this world, but we will be recompensed in Heaven where perfect love reigns.

Have you ever noticed in your own life or while watching another going through trials that we try to shift the blame to someone else when we are not overcoming? "It's their fault that I'm behaving the way I am." Some pretend that they can't keep from sinning. "It is just too hard!" "I don't have the will power!" "The devil made me do it!" "My wife, (or my husband) made me angry!" The problem is, they almost sound as though God is in agreement with their sinful actions. Have you ever tried to justify your sin? If there is any sinful issue in the heart of someone or the sinful conduct in their life, it cannot, nor ever will be attributed to God. He is not the author of sin; He just exposes it.

Tried, But Not Destroyed

James 1:13-15 *Let no man say when he is tempted, I am tempted of God: for God cannot be tempted with evil, neither tempteth he any man: But every man is tempted, when he is drawn away of his own lust, and enticed. Then when lust hath conceived, it bringeth forth sin: and sin, when it is finished, bringeth forth death.*

Trials are allowed to come into a Christian's life because the Lord wants to draw out all the evil in our hearts. The Father deeply desires that we become like Jesus. Many times the only way this can be accomplished is for the believer to go through tough times. Evil and temptation have their origins in our own hearts.

When we become first saved, we often adopt a "Tiptoe Through the Tulips" attitude. We think we have made it now! Our lives will be a bed of roses. We have this misconception and that the devil will leave us alone and will never bother us again. If this is your experience as a Christian, I would question your faithfulness and walk with the Lord. The closer our walk with Jesus, the more we desire to do His work and serve Him, the more the devil comes to torment us. If you aren't being bombarded with attacks of the devil, then you aren't working hard enough for the Lord...you're not a threat to Satan's kingdom. Now don't misunderstand what I'm saying here. We are overcomers. We have the Blood of the Lamb, which cleanses us from all unrighteousness. Satan doesn't like us getting people saved, healing the sick, raising the dead, teaching people the Word of God, preaching, prophesying, building churches, and speaking truth. The Lord will allow the enemy to test us for a season so that together with the Lord, we will root out all evil thoughts, pride, control, manipulation, rebellion, etc. Why is this necessary? The reason is because the Lord is forming and molding us to His own image.

As we continue to strive to be that overcomer to receive the crown of life in eternity, blessings will come from the Lord. A Christian who overcomes the enemy by the Blood of the Lamb becomes a different

173

person from what he was before receiving the Lord's grace.

Eternal life with the Lord is ours. Not everyone who suffers is blessed. (Unbelievers and Christians who give up and give in.) However, all of us who endure with patience and perseverance, and make it through all the difficulties all the way to the end, shall be crowned with the *Crown of Life*.

A Christian who endures trials will be crowned with a promise.

As ministers of Christ, we will have demands and commands from Him that we are that we are expected to fulfill. The Lord will allow your heart to be tried and show you your sin. The trials you go through will reveal your true heart. It will be exposed. God will reveal the corruption, sin, and evil in our hearts. Every man has sin, because of his fleshly lusts.

James 1:12-18 ***Blessed is the man that endureth temptation: for when he is tried, he shall receive the crown of life, which the Lord hath promised to them that love him.*** *Let no man say when he is tempted, I am tempted of God: for God cannot be tempted with evil, neither tempteth he any man: But every man is tempted, when he is drawn away of his own lust, and enticed. Then when lust hath conceived, it bringeth forth sin: and sin, when it is finished, bringeth forth death. Do not err, my beloved brethren.* ***Every good gift and every perfect gift is from above,*** *and cometh down from the Father*

174

of lights, with whom is no variableness, neither shadow of turning. Of his own will begat he us with the word of truth, that we should be a kind of firstfruits of his creatures.

Being born again is our best good gift from God. As the Scripture says, "Every good gift and every perfect gift is from above." Because of the grace He bestows on us, if we rejoice in that grace we will stay happy in the Lord. Be the firstfruits of His creatures.

Revelation 2:10-11 *Fear none of those things which thou shalt suffer: behold, the devil shall cast some of you into prison, that ye may be tried; and ye shall have tribulation ten days: <u>be thou faithful unto death, and I will give thee a crown of life</u>. He that hath an ear, let him hear what the Spirit saith unto the churches; He that overcometh shall not be hurt of the second death.*

The Word of God says to fear none of those things that you shall suffer. If you can be faithful even unto death, then the Lord will give you a crown of life. Here on earth, there will always be trials and troubles. But remember, we are *not to fear.* Jesus is the First and Last, and He is a Judge of us all.

Revelation 22:13 *I am Alpha and Omega, the beginning and the end, the first and the last.*

Notice the Word of God says we are tried, not destroyed. The Lord also says, "I will give thee..." The reward of the crown of life will be given to us from Christ's own hand. Think about it. When we receive the crown of life, which is eternal life, how much greater reward could there be? As we go through life, sometimes feeling worn out in the Lord's service, we

175

must remember that we will be rewarded with a much better afterlife with our Lord. As we overcome the devil, He promises that we will not be hurt of the second death. The second death is to be always dying and not receiving eternal life.

<u>*As a believer in Jesus Christ,*</u>
<u>*you will not be destroyed.*</u>
<u>*You will only be tried in your faith.*</u>

Remember, we choose whether to receive His hope of eternal salvation accompanied by the crown of life.

1 Thessalonians 3:12-13 *And the Lord make you to increase and abound in love one toward another, and toward all men, even as we do toward you: <u>To the end he may stablish your hearts unblameable in holiness before God</u>, even our Father, at the coming of our Lord Jesus Christ with all his saints.*

176

Chapter 16

Golden Crown

Revelation 14:14-15 *And I looked, and behold a white cloud, and upon the cloud one sat like unto the Son of man, having on his head a <u>golden crown</u>, and in his hand a sharp sickle. And another angel came out of the temple, crying with a loud voice to him that sat on the cloud, Thrust in thy sickle, and reap: for <u>the time is come for thee to reap; for the harvest of the earth is ripe.</u>*

At the time of the Lord's appearing, an Angel of the Lord will be wearing a golden crown. The golden crown represents authority. A pure authority. A righteous authority. The gold crowns cited in the Bible and described throughout history were very intricately and exquisitely designed. The crown was to be worn with honor and dignity. It was also a sign of royalty. In the spiritual realm, this Angel of the Lord will demonstrate his loyalty, honor, royalty, and authority. This Angel has the boldness and power of the Lord to carry out the plan of the Father.

Harvest Time

The time of harvest is near. When the harvest is reaped with the soon-coming arrival of our King, Christ will begin to separate His faithful from the unfaithful, the fruitful from the unfruitful. Just as a farmer comes to harvest his crops, in like manner the Lord will come to reap His reward—His children. During this time of harvest, many Christians will have been persecuted and martyred for the Lord. They will receive the greatest reward, the Crown of Life - eternal life with the Lord. We are to not fear this separation, but rather rejoice in it. The Lord Jesus Christ promises us that we will pass from death to life.

> **John 5:24** *Verily, verily, I say unto you, He that heareth my word, and believeth on him that sent me, hath everlasting life, and shall not come into condemnation; but is passed from death unto life.*

In Revelation 14:15, another angel comes and yells to the one wearing the golden crown, *"Thrust in thy sickle, and reap: ...the harvest of the earth is ripe."* This statement refers to the time of the end. The end of the earth as we know it. By this time the warnings and judgments of God have already occurred.

Presently, there are many people on earth who have not repented and accepted Jesus as Lord. The harvest is a gathering, a gathering of the wheat. Christians are the wheat. The Lord gives many warnings and calls to righteousness. Many warnings are being cried out in our land right now.

The unrighteous and wicked will be destroyed. The Scripture speaks of a winepress. This winepress signifies the wrath of God. As believers we are promised that we won't see the wrath of God. However, we will experience the warnings and judgments.

How can we know that we will be protected from seeing the wrath of God? What about the warnings and judgments of God? Why do we have to go through these trials and tribulations? I certainly don't have all the answers, but of one thing I am certain: that God's ways are higher than ours. He says He will never leave us nor forsake us. He also says in His Word that we will be victorious, and we are overcomers.

Many have speculated about whether or not September 11, 2001 was a judgment from God. Obviously the Lord allowed the attack, but I believe it was a warning. A judgment from the Lord is much harsher and more devastating. Remember the account in the Word about the destruction of Sodom and Gomorrah? What about Noah, the ark and the flood? Sodom and Gomorrah and all the cities of the plains were destroyed. In the days of Noah, the whole earth was covered by the flood. As a parent, sometimes I give warnings to my children and others call for sentences, or judgments. Warning is a possible way out of the consequences of sin for my children, but judgment is the actual act of discipline and is not optional. They cannot get out of judgment.

There is so much filth in our country today. When you watch TV, the dads are portrayed as though they are really stupid. The moms are given no respect. The children are having sex, cursing, and getting away with whatever they want. The wives on TV and in the movies want to be the heads of companies, their homes, and over the men they're in relationship with. Women belittle and betray the men. Men and women are only looking to see who they can have sex with that particular night. Even the names of the TV shows reflect how it is in our society..."Sex and the City."

I could continue to mention all the things wrong with the world, but what about us, the Christians, the Church? Is there a little bit of the world in each one of us? How far do we let it get out of hand? Are there righteous men and women to be found in our midst?

As I was listening to a Christian radio program one day, I was shown just exactly how ignorant Christians are about the Endtimes. A well-known ministry broadcast this program. Two men hosting the show and taking calls were asked a question: "Where is America in Bible prophecy? The answer that these men gave actually shocked me. One hadn't even considered the question prior to this, and the other one stated, "We are a nation blessed by God. There are so many Christians in this nation that when we are gone (meaning in the rapture), there won't be very many people even left in this nation. Therefore, it must not have been worth mentioning (in the Bible) because it won't matter anymore."

What? There are so many Christians in this nation? Just because many in this country call themselves Christian doesn't mean that they are. Most Americans believe they are a Christian just because they live in the U.S. We are so deceived - our hearts deceive us. We have become a Nation filled with compromise and corruption. The whole world looks at us and sees hypocrites. We have such a haughty spirit and think we're so great that we're actually allowing the spirit of Babylon to rule us.

(Read Jeremiah, Chapters 50 and 51; Revelation, Chapter 18; and Isaiah, Chapter 13 to learn about America's fate in the Word.)

In Sodom and Gomorrah, evidently Lot was a good enough man in God's eyes to have his life spared. Yet, remember, there was not even one other person found to be in the same category as Lot. All the people were very wicked and evil. There were homosexuals, molesters, adulterers, and so forth. The character of Lot is similar to those of many Christians today. Lot was taking his time getting out of Sodom and Gomorah. He lingered there. That is exactly what many Christians do. When we come under the conviction of the Holy Spirit, many of us ignore the prompting to change. We have salvation through grace and mercy of the Lord. Praise the Lord that we cannot become good enough to receive His salvation. We would never make it.

Remember, Lot had to flee out of Sodom. He had to run for his life and was commanded to not look back. This is exactly what the Lord tells us to do. We are never to return to sin. We are not to allow Satan to rule and reign in our life. We are to repent—turn away from sin and walk the other way. Our eyes need to be fixed on heaven and the new earth, not the one we're on right now. Judgment can lead to total destruction, but His children can be spared. Most assuredly, we will be spared from His wrath. Hallelujah!

The Peace of God

When the attack of September 11, 2001 occurred, Stan, our two youngest children, Bentley and Leslie Ann, and I were in New York City. A few days earlier we had finished conducting *The Power of Jesus Crusades* in Albany, New York. We decided to take a few extra days off afterward with the children to see New York City, since none of us had ever been there before. On Monday, September 10th, we drove to New York City. We arrived about 6:30 p.m. Our first thought was to find a place to eat and get a hotel room. We had planned to get up early the next morning, head to downtown Manhattan, and buy some of those famous bagels we hear so much about. As we were coming into the city, all of a sudden we changed our plans. We all wanted to drive downtown Manhattan that evening and see Times Square. We thought maybe we might even be able to find hotel accommodations in the city.

We didn't know any better, but I guess no sane person would volunteer to drive downtown Manhattan. I was the one driving the rental car with my family. They just kept squirming and covering their eyes. I thought it was fun, and I got just as aggressive as the best of them. We drove around for a couple of hours, viewing the Empire State Building and Times Square. We stopped several places trying to find a place to stay overnight. Imagine this, there was *"no room at the Inn."* We tried probably five different hotels. Not one of them had any room for us. We then decided to find someplace to park so we could walk up and down Times Square. We got something to eat and just walked and looked around until about 11:00 p.m.

Since we hadn't been able to find a place to stay, we decided to head back under the bridge to the New Jersey side and stay there for the night. Our plan still was to get up early the next morning and head back to Manhattan. We were going to see on foot the World Trade Center and the Empire State Building. We found a hotel four miles from the World Trade Center. Drifting off to sleep I prayed, "Lord, we have had very little sleep, and we have been working really hard. Would you let us get a good night's sleep and even sleep in longer than usual tomorrow. I know Stan wants to get up early, but we're all so tired." With that prayer, we all conked out!

The other thing that is significant is that I turned my cell phone off before I went to sleep. When we are out of town, I always leave it on during the night in case anyone would need to reach us. The next morning we woke up around 9:30 a.m. I reached for my cell phone, and when I turned it on there were seven messages. I began to listen to the messages, and the first one was from our son, Shawn, in Topeka. The message was, "Mom, are you all okay? Call me. I am worried about you. A plane just crashed into the World Trade Center, and I know you were going to be there this morning. Call me mom; I am so worried." With that, I immediately turned on the TV. There it was, only four miles from us, the devastation of the attack on the World Trade Center. My husband, Leslie Ann and Bentley ran outside. Right across the bay, the World Trade Center was surrounded by smoke.

While watching TV, I saw the second plane crash. It was awful, and I began to panic. I quickly took a shower, praying the whole time and began packing furiously. I just wanted to get out of there. I had to take a deep breath and cry out for the peace of God. All of a sudden I felt that peace which passes all understanding fall on me. I quit talking and just waited on the Lord. He said, "Daughter, recognize My peace. I have not put this fear on you. Do not look at the circumstance; remember the peace I give to you." Then I remembered what I had prayed before going to sleep the night before; that we would sleep in later than normal and not wake up early. The Lord revealed to me that here in the midst of the

182

horrific destruction going on all around us, that He had us resting and in peace. There were sirens, alarms, horns honking, people yelling up and down the halls, and chaos going on all around us, yet we were sleeping soundly. He showed me that even through this terrible disaster, this warning for our country, we had His presence around us.

We left New Jersey as quickly as we could with no idea how to get home. We had rented a car so we decided we would just drive back to Topeka. There was no way we were going to get a flight out of New Jersey the next morning. We headed down a main highway and all began to pray. "Lord, we don't know what highway we are supposed to be on. We don't even know what direction to go in. Please, Holy Spirit, guide and direct us." About that time, we came to a toll road. When we got to the toll-booth, Stan told the man, "We want to go to Topeka, Kansas. Which way do we go?" Can you believe this? The man told Stan the directions, and off we went. For two days, we did nothing but drive and listen to the news on the radio.

On the second day of driving, I remember looking in the back seat at Leslie Ann and Bentley. They were playing cards and laughing, having a great time! Here I was starting to get a little depressed because of all the terrible news reports, and my children were laughing. I sought the Lord's view of this. "Why is it that Leslie Ann and Bentley are so calm? Don't they know what's going on?" The Spirit of the Lord spoke so graciously to me. He said, "Daughter, they have My peace. Remember, even through the sirens, the horns, and the devastation, I gave you rest, and I gave you directions home. This is how it will be in the future for My children who are with Me and following My commandments." I was overwhelmed with His peace once again and began to weep, because I knew that my Lord had just given us such grace and mercy. He spared our lives, and even through the devastation and destruction He gave us rest.

What a lesson we can all learn from this! If we rest in the Lord, if we stay clean and righteous before Him, He will protect His own. I guarantee that even those who knew the Lord and lost their lives that day received His peace when they needed it the most. I'm sure He reached out His hand

183

to greet each one of them and take them into His presence.

We can remain calm and joyful no matter what the circumstances are if we stay in the strength and confidence of the Lord. His salvation brings us joy. We will advance in God's Kingdom if we trust and obey Him. All the blessings the Lord bestows on us are due to His goodness and mercy. We don't receive because of anything we do - through no merit of our own.

The Lord many times gives us blessings even before we pray for them, even, sometimes, before we're ready for them. He goes before us and is our Rear Guard. In our case, He actually even prevented us from experiencing the disaster firsthand. The Lord is so good that He even allowed us to see downtown Manhattan before the roads were closed off, before the warning of 9/11.

What we need to pray is that the warnings and judgments will produce reformation, before it is too late for America. The cup of the sins of the world is full and overflowing. We are ripe for judgment. There is a time on the calendar of God when the sinners, the unbelievers, will be ripe for the harvest. There will come a time when the Lord will not spare them any longer and they will be ruined.

Our Lord not only has an incredible amount of patience with His children who sin against Him, but toward the ungodly as well.

Prayer for the Lord's Protection

Lord, we desire that our whole families would be saved—that the ungodly will turn from their wicked ways and repent. Lord, it says in your Word that our whole household will be saved. We desire, proclaim, and declare that the <u>place your family name here</u> will know you as their Lord and Savior. We desire your blessings and goodness for our lives. We know that we will receive a crown of pure gold at the moment of

Your appearing. We do not want any of our loved ones to be lost and go through your wrath. Remove the bondages. Remove the blinders from their spiritual eyes. Remove the earplugs from their spiritual ears. Let us all and our loved ones hear what the Spirit of the Lord is saying to His children. In the days of warnings and judgments, let us have peace - the peace that passes **all** understanding. You say when to go to the right or left, we will know what direction to take. We will not react in fear but allow the presence of the Lord to rule in our life. Thank you for saving us. Thank You for delivering us. Thank You for your promises and blessings.

In Jesus' Name, Amen!

Prayer to be Prayed Each Day!

Dear Heavenly Father,

I come to you in the name of Jesus. I adore you and worship you. You are my Master, my Savior, my Lord, and King. I ask forgiveness for my sins and the sins of my family. I remit the sins of my forefathers and put them under the Blood of Jesus.

I put on the full armor of God now, the helmet of salvation, my righteous breastplate, the girdle of truth, and the shield of faith. I have the sword of the Spirit and my feet shod with the gospel of peace. I am standing on the Word, the Word of God.

I plead the Blood of Jesus over my spirit, soul, and body; over my family members and loved ones. I plead the Blood of Jesus over my property and the ministry you have me in. I plead the blood of Jesus over my finances, and I declare that I am debt-free. I plead the Blood of Jesus over my health and mind - the conscious, subconscious, and sub-liminal areas.

I ask, Lord of hosts, for You to place your minister-ing and guardian angels all around me and my family. I ask that you send forth your angels, your reapers, to bring in the promises and blessings from You Lord.

I ask that You bless me indeed, that You would en-large my coast, keep Your hand upon me and keep me from evil and doing evil.

Lord, I thank You for what you are doing in my life. Thank You that my whole household is saved and serving you.

In Jesus' name. Amen!

The Lord doesn't want us to be feeling condemnation about sin in our lives, rather the Holy Spirit convicts us and we ask for forgiveness and repent. Do not allow the enemy to come into your thoughts and make you doubt about your salvation or, for that matter, that the Lord could or would never forgive you, but rather praise the Lord for loving you so much He gives you grace and mercy. The Lord Jesus Christ does love you and wants you to receive His Crown of Glory and Honor. It will be a beautiful crown of pure transparent gold with the most precious gem-stones.

Remember, the Lord wants to bless you with His crowns. Receive salvation through Jesus Christ as Lord and have eternal life.

Psalms 21:3 *For thou preventest him with the blessings of goodness: thou settest a crown of pure gold on his head.*

Being righteous, holy, and clean is the key to receiving His Crowns!

Here we are, another chapter - another book finished in your life. I would like to leave you with this story. Stan asked a question to a young lady, Katrina, who was wearing a crown promoting her title, Miss Capital City. He inquired, "Do people treat you differently when you are wearing the crown?" She thought for a moment and then replied, "Of course they do. But, I am also different when I am wearing the crown. I am more poised, confident, stand up straighter; I know how to act in public. I am very aware of good manners and I make sure others feel important." Katrina also said, "Maybe I should just pretend this crown is on my head all the time. If I were to envision this crown on my head when I go in for a job interview, there would be not way they would turn me down. I could get the job and probably ask and receive a raise before I even started working."

If we as Christians began at this moment visualizing the different crowns on our heads, just think how differently we would act and react to things. It would be a constant reminder that we certainly need to be humble, gracious, courageous, clean, virtuous, kind, etc. It reminds me of the Scripture;

> **Philippians 4:8-9** *Finally, brethren, whatsoever things are true, whatsoever things are honest, whatsoever things are just, whatsoever things are pure, whatsoever things are lovely, whatsoever things are of good report; if there be any virtue, and if there be any praise, think on these things. Those things, which ye have both learned, and received, and heard, and seen in me, do: and the God of peace shall be with you.*

The crowns we believe we receive and know spiritually are ours, the more we will become Christlike day-by-day.

Believe it, Receive it!

About The Author

Leslie Johnson is Founder of the nationwide radio program and Women's Conference *The Perfect Touch*. She is also the Co-founder of **The Power of Jesus Crusades** which are held monthly all across America.

Leslie teaches about intercession, praise and worship, and ministers in and demonstrates the power of Jesus. Leslie has been involved in ministry for over 16 years and was formally ordained on May 7, 2000.

Since then, God has directed her to write books pertaining to what God has done in her life. Leslie is in great demand as a speaker at conferences, seminars, and intercessory groups across the globe. She walks in the anointing of the Holy Spirit and is in the office of prophet.

Leslie's deepest desire is to see God's people set free, delivered, and able to walk in holiness and righteousness.

For more information concerning the following:

* Additional copies of this book

* To schedule speaking engagements

* The radio program

* *The Power of Jesus Crusades!*

* The Prophecy Club® Magazine

You may contact Leslie at:

Leslie Johnson
c/o Spirit of Prophecy Church
P. O. Box 750234
Topeka, KS 66675

or

e-mail: lesliej@cjnetworks.com
or
Phone: 785-266-1112
Fax: 785-266-6200